Sew Adorkable

15 DIY Projects to Keep You Out of Trouble

Quilts, Clothes & Gear for the Chic Geek

Samarra Khaja

stash BOOKS.

an imprint of C&T Publishing

Text and artwork copyright © 2015 by Samarra Khaja

Photography copyright © 2015 by C&T Publishing, Inc.

Publisher: Amy Marson

Creative Director: Gailen Runge

Art Director/Book Designer:
Kristy Zacharias

Editor: S. Michele Fry

Technical Editors: Doreen Hazel
and Nanette Zeller

Production Coordinator:
Freesia Pearson Blizard

Production Editor: Alice Mace Nakanishi

Illustrator: Samarra Khaja

Photo Assistant: Mary Peyton Peppo

Style photography by Nissa Brehmer
and instructional photography by
Diane Pedersen, unless otherwise noted

Published by Stash Books, an imprint of C&T Publishing, Inc., P.O. Box 1456,
Lafayette, CA 94549

Library of Congress Cataloging-in-Publication Data

Khaja, Samarra, 1971-

 Sew adorkable : 15 DIY projects to keep you out of trouble--quilts, clothes &
gear for the chic geek / Samarra Khaja.

     pages cm

  ISBN 978-1-61745-057-0 (soft cover)

1. Dress accessories--Patterns. 2. Tailoring--Patterns. 3. Patchwork quilts.
I. Title.

TT649.8.K44 2015

646'.3--dc23

                              2015005323

Printed in China

10 9 8 7 6 5 4 3 2 1

Contents

Dedication

I owe a debt of gratitude to my beloved Jack, Kip, and Ren for being there for me throughout the making of this book, much like Olympic gymnastics spotters or elite racing pit crews. (Let's face it, they didn't have much choice, really—although they could have changed the locks on the house, I suppose.) Without their endless love, support, feedback, cheerleading, and enthusiasm, I wouldn't have made it to the finish line as quasi-gracefully as I did. Oh, and thanks for letting me turn the house into an unmitigated disaster zone. Much love to my endlessly supportive mom and dad and especially to Aman for being there to make me see the world with more patience, humanity, and understanding. This book is for these beautiful people … and for Baby Otto. Can't forget the family pet fish.

Acknowledgments

My head would have combusted if it weren't also for these great people who helped make my drawing, sewing, and creating much more fun: *Hayden* (you got me into this mess!) and all the great folks at Timeless Treasures for aiding and abetting my fabric hoarding tendencies. Also a big thanks to Singer (*Vanessa!*), Pellon (*Erin!*), Dritz (*Paula!*), AccuQuilt (*Loretta!*), Clover (*Raquel!*), Olfa (*Robin!*), Wacom (*Pam!*), Oliso (*Scott!*), and Aurifil (*Alex!*)—all of whom I'm extremely proud to partner with. I've always believed in good-quality products that actually walk the walk, and all these brands hit that mark, plus they've got cute-to-look-at stuff that makes my work flow extra fun and enjoyable.

Thanks to Jeannie Jenkins, my go-to longarm quilter, whose beautiful work can be admired on both my *Candy Dots* and *Braille Alphabet* quilts. Also to Oona and Irina for their mad sewing skills when I didn't have enough hands to do everything myself.

And finally, a monumental thank you to all my collaborators in crime at C&T / Stash Books (that means you, *Roxane! Gailen! Michele! Doreen! Kristy! Nissa!*). It has been an immense pleasure to drag you talented bunch along my crazy craft ride.

Introduction

Well, now you've done it.

Here you were, minding your own business, searching for a first edition of *A Concise History of Thumb Wrestling*, and now look ... you went and picked up THIS book along the way. Well to that I say, in a too-loud, sing-songy, musical theater voice, "H-e-l-l-o, unforeseeable SCORE!"

Let us rejoice and dance in a festive circle; sure, sure, you can bring out that travel-size maypole you carry around in your bag for emergency situations like this.

Once we're fully winded (way sooner than we should be), let's stop and find out what the heck this book is really about, shall we?

Game on.

Here's the deal. You and I both know there is a lot of seriousness in sewing, but what there's not enough of is humor. Good old-fashioned foolishness and shameless punniness on a grand DIY scale.

And *that* is why this book is here!

[Anthropomorphized book with sequined spats and top hat enters stage left, grinning profusely, while sidestepping across the stage; jazz hands optional.]

This book is for smart, talented, crafty folks (I'm lookin' straight at you) who have an eye for whimsy and who love good tongue-in-cheek visual play. The projects included are all conversation starters that celebrate those strong-willed sewers out there who want not only something handmade but also something unique. These projects please the eye and complement the sofa, and as a bonus they say so much about the person who makes them—a true expression of the creator's whim.

So what's in store for you when it comes to these projects? I'm glad you asked, my good friend.

You'll find cleverly themed projects that aren't subject to cultural and gender lines and that can be adapted to suit children and adults alike. They totally debunk traditional ideas of what's exclusively for young versus old or girls versus boys. In this book, we don't care about those delineations, because humor and fun transcend all boundaries. And let's face it—we all love a good laugh and to be surrounded by things that make us happy.

Along with morsels of silliness, educational tidbits are added for extra flavor whenever possible. You can admire the ingenuity and brilliance of Louis Braille while sewing up a queen-size quilted ode to his alphabet. And you can pay homage to one of the many dinosaurs that once walked Earth while piecing together amusing family portraits that no house is complete without. Seriously people, I implore you to make many and line the stairs with them.

Take this book (pay for it first; we're not a bunch of hooligans), go home, get your materials, and get making—you smart, hilarious, creative creature, you.

Behind the Seams:

Tale of a Textile Designer

"What do you do?" Easy enough question, but my answer is quite hard to fully present in its real-to-life form. That said, let's take a paltry stab at showing you a bit of my textile designing world, shall we?

The Ideas

Here's the thing: Much like a moth to a flame, I cannot resist a good paradox. With the precision of a truffle-sniffing pig, my brain will, nine times out of ten, fling itself directly into one, pinpointing the extraordinary in the ordinary or the ordinary within the extraordinary. Narrowing in on these paradoxes fuels my sense of humor, and because I like to laugh, it's a chronic occurrence.

This predisposition frames my visual sensibility and inevitably leads me to doing things like taking an idiom and twisting it from metaphoric to literal, as with my When Pigs Fly fabric (page 47). The unexpected within the expected surfaces in designs like my Hidden Ladybugs fabric (page 10). I adore taking the sensible and mundane in life and angling it just enough to reveal the absurd and offbeat. Whether by way of changing scale, tapping into childhood nostalgia or time-honored traditions, or playing with technique and presentation, my cherished love of paradox is a loud, cacophonous running theme throughout this book. I hope you like it, because it's hard to miss.

Black
and White
Animals

The Process

My designs are all hand drawn in one way or another. Some begin on good old-fashioned paper—I like vellum, in particular—with pen or pencil. Others come to life directly on my Wacom Cintiq—my tablet companion. Once I've refined my concepts, they all make their way into Adobe Illustrator, my preferred graphic design software, where I finesse the repeat and select my color palette. I typically find hints of specific colors while I'm out and about in my daily life (the aqua blue pool at my kids' swimming lessons, for example). I tend to choose bright, bold colors.

Once I've sorted out a pleasing combination of colors, I adjust my file accordingly and send it off for proofing. After not too long, I receive a strike-off, which is the first test version of that design printed onto fabric. I examine the swatch, checking it for scale, flow, and color. Sometimes colors need further adjusting; sometimes everything's perfect as is and ready to sign off.

After my approval, the fabric moves on to production and, later, release and distribution. It never gets old seeing a finished design when it debuts and knowing the artistic journey behind its creation. From my brain to printed bolt and topped off with my selvage signature—it's an addictively fun ride.

My original New York City skyline drawing, inked on vellum, alongside the final printed fabric version, Great Gotham

One of my original pencil sketches for Imagine That, alongside the finished printed version. This was my very first fabric design to debut, so it's a sentimental favorite.

Whoosh! Did You See That?

Like the fabric flip-book equivalent of a lightning-paced game of "I Spy," you may spot some of my fabric designs making cameo appearances throughout this book. (They're unruly beasties—each one jumping up and down, waving its warps and wefts this way and that, trying to out-spotlight the others. I've taught them better, but sometimes they have minds of their own.) In each project's materials list, I note my fabric by name and with a picture. You're certainly free to choose something different, but I can tell you that the wild-children fabrics would love to be a part of your life.

Clothing

Fabrics

Fireworks

Thumbprint Owls

Confetti Polka Dots

Stained Glass

TRAWRzers!

You know when you stand in front of your dresser for what seems like days, trying to decide what on prehistoric Earth you should wear? Well, before you're once again mysteriously drawn to those unsightly, baggy-bottomed track pants (why do you do this to yourself?), step up your fashion ferociousness and get some TRAWRzers into wild rotation for a roaring good time!

fun facts

Sure, we're focused on dinosaur-inspired pants here, but have you ever pondered pants for dinosaurs? Let's pretend for a minute that a T-Rex walked into our tailoring shop (yes, we have a tailoring shop together). If we measured from his hip to ankle, we might get 4 yards, and if we measured all the way around his hips, we might get about 7 yards. Shake that all up together with a few added computations, and we'd realize we need about 30 whopping yards of fabric to make his pants. The upswing of this newfound fabric flood is that he did not ask for reversible overalls. Not yet.

What You'll Need

- **Dinosaur scale patterns** (page 17)

- **Assorted fabric:** for dinosaur scales

- **Samarra's fabrics (see below):** for pants and scales

Confetti Polka Dots (for pants)

Thumbprint Owls (for pants)

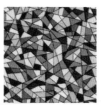
Stained Glass (for scales)

It's Go Time!

Side seam allowances on the dinosaur scales are ½". The pants side seam allowance should match the manufactured pants seam or the size specified by the pattern.

1. Make a pair of lounge pants from your favorite pattern or use a store-bought pair of pants; we're totally cool with quasi-homemade projects here. This is a sewing safe place, ducklings, not to worry.

- If you're making your own, follow all construction steps but stop before sewing the outer leg seams together.

- If you're starting with a store-bought pair, use your best friend, the seam ripper, to unpick the outer seams of each pant leg from just above the ankle cuff area to just below the hip/waist/pocket area.

Set aside.

2. Determine how many scales you want on both legs. Using any one of the scale patterns, cut out that number times 2 (you need a front and a back for each scale).

> ### Tip
>
> Pick a uniformly sized and shaped scale, mix things up with a combination of different scales, or consider using a range of gradient colors or fabric patterns for endless TRAWRzer variations.

3. Take a pair of scale shapes and place them right sides together. Sew together with a ½" seam, leaving the bottom edge open.

4. Snip off excess fabric near the points of the scale shape. Turn right side out. Use a rounded-end pointed tool to make crisp points. Iron the shape flat.

5. Repeat Steps 3 and 4 with the remaining scale shapes.

All Together Now

Turn the pants inside out and lay them flat. Insert each scale shape along the outer leg seam, aligning the raw edges of the scales and the pants side seams. Evenly space scales along each pant leg. Pin the scales in place.

Almost Done!

1. Pin the top layer of pants fabric over the pinned scales and the bottom layer of pants fabric, so the pants side seams match at the raw edge.

2. Sew up the outer seam of each pant leg from the waistline to the cuff, following the pants pattern instructions for a seam allowance. For store-bought pants, sew along the original seamline.

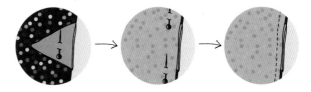

3. Finish any remaining pants sewing steps according to the pattern instructions.

> ### Tip
>
> **Don't be selfish and keep these gloRAWRious pants just for your private quarters. Take a page out of the book of any kid and wear them proudly to the store to pick out your vittles and veggies, you crazy animal, you! Oooh, why not turn a pair into the ultimate tuxedo pants ever to exist? Just use fine black suiting fabric and luscious black satin to soup up your game to prowler perfection!**

Ta-Dah!

We are RAWRall done! Your daily clothing quandaries have been solved, giving you much more time to drink coffee in the morning. Scale up or down and make a wild pair for each and every wild beast in that ferociously fashionable family of yours.

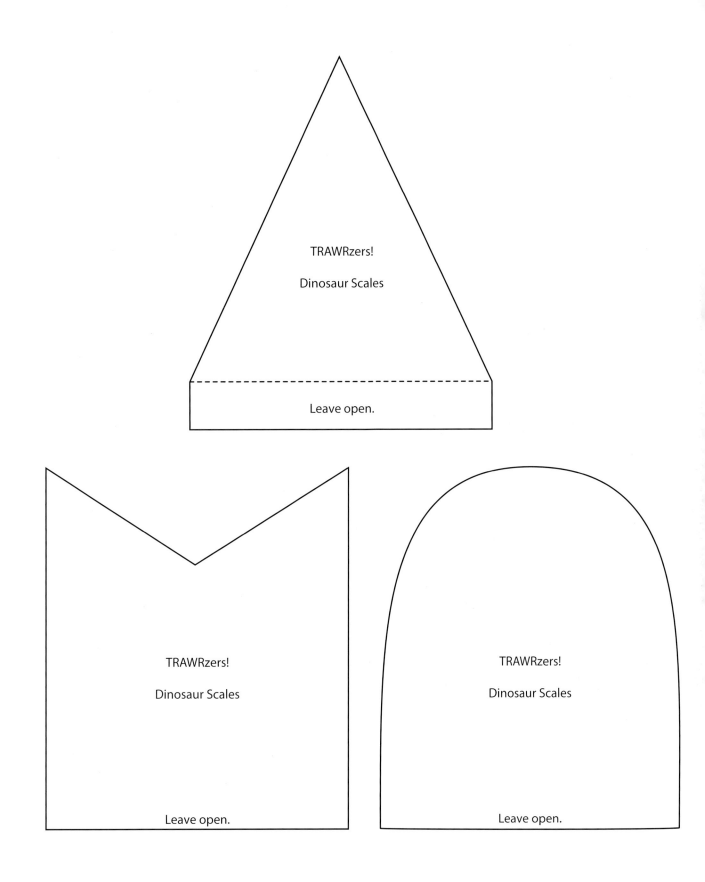

TRAWRzers!

Dinosaur Scales

Leave open.

TRAWRzers!

Dinosaur Scales

Leave open.

TRAWRzers!

Dinosaur Scales

Leave open.

Meta Pencil Skirt

Finished appliqué size: approximately 6¾″ × 18¼″

Office clothes can be so incredibly dull, boring, and downright ugly. As if it's not miserable enough to be cooped up in a cubicle doing something that's not what you dreamed of in college, the available options for business attire don't help. So what better way to lift your mood—because the recirculated air won't—and add some joy to your *is-it-time-to-go-home-yet?* workday than combining two office classics into one ultimate, self-referential clothing classic—the Meta Pencil Skirt.

fun facts

Lead *it be known that standard writing pencils contain no lead. Rather they contain varying ratios of graphite and clay mixed together. Colored pencils are made up of mixtures of pigment with varying levels of gums, resins, and wax that act as binding agents. Both types come in different qualities and grades.*

There's even a nonprofit organization called the Colored Pencil Society of America— yup, you heard me right—that's dedicated to promoting colored pencils as a fine-art medium. And with that, you may now consider your pencil knowledge fully sharpened.

What You'll Need

- **Pencil tip patterns** (page 23)
- **Cherry red fabric:** ⅛ yard for pencil A

  Cut 1 rectangle A1 3¼″ × 13″.
- **Light brown fabric:** ⅛ yard for pencil B

  Cut 1 rectangle B1 3¼″ × 16″.
- **Gray fabric:** ⅛ yard for pencil C

  Cut 1 rectangle C1 3¼″ × 12″.

- **Tan fabric:** about 3″ × 7½″ for large pencil tips (pencil "wood")
- **Paper-backed fusible webbing**
- **Tear-away stabilizer**
- **Template paper**

> **Tip**
>
> One of the most fun things about projects like this is the option to truly personalize your design. Choose a sophisticated color palette or go for something more chirpy and bright—this design works both ways. Young or old, festive or subdued, mix and match as you like to create a really unique statement. And don't forget a sweet novelty print as a pencil option, too. Ahem, you catch my drift.

It's Go Time!

Appliqué seam allowances are ½″ for this project.

1. Make a pencil skirt from your favorite pattern or use a store-bought pencil skirt, 'cuz hey, nobody's gonna judge you here. If making one from scratch, follow all the pattern instructions and stop before the hemming step. If you store buy, unpick the hem. Set the skirt aside.

> **Tip**
>
> For child-size skirts, reduce the appliqué pattern to fit, shrinking it down to 75 percent or 50 percent, depending on the skirt size.

2. Trace the Small Pencil Tip pattern onto paper-backed fusible web. Make 3, leaving space between each. Roughly cut out the shapes. Iron the fusible webbing shapes to the back of each remaining piece of the 3 pencil fabrics (cherry, light brown, and gray). Cut out the 3 small triangles along the tracing lines (pencil tips A3, B3, and C3).

3. Trace the Large Pencil Tip pattern onto template paper. Use it to cut out pencil tip triangles A2, B2, and C2, from the tan fabric. (I did not add webbing to the backs of these pieces, but you can if you prefer.)

4. Iron and fuse pieces A3, B3, and C3 to the top point of pieces A2, B2, and C2, respectively.

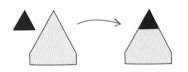

5. Use coordinating thread to satin stitch a line along the bottom edge of each newly positioned A3, B3, and C3 piece.

6. Center and sew each of these fused pencil tips atop their corresponding rectangle pieces to create each pencil A, B, and C. Note that the rectangles are wider to allow for seams. Press the seam toward the rectangle.

All Together Now

1. Adjust the lengths of the A1, B1, and C1 rectangles to suit the individual skirt size and how tall/short the pencils will be when finished. The top finished edge of rectangle A1 should sit 3″ lower than rectangle B1, and rectangle C1 should sit 4″ lower than rectangle B1. Leave the uneven bottom edges to be trimmed later.

2. Using a ½″ seam allowance, sew assembled pencil A to pencil B and pencil B to pencil C, following the top edge spacing measurements from Step 1. Press the seams open.

3. Note the ½″ overhang on the left edge of A1 and the right edge of C1. Fold each overhang ½″ under and iron flat to create a finished edge along each side. The appliqué is now fully assembled and is ready to attach to the pencil skirt.

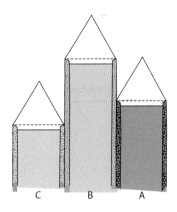

Tip

An appliqué can be attached to a backing fabric in a number of ways. In this case, I used a piece of tear-away stabilizer all by itself on the wrong side of the skirt fabric, because I'm crazy like that. If you want extra assurance that your appliqué will lie flat and stay in place before final stitching, consider using a fusible webbing, such as Pellon Wonder-Under, on the back of the appliqué. If you choose to do that, now's the time to add that sandwiching step.

Almost Done!

1. With the skirt lying flat, front side up, decide which side the pencils will go on, along with how high or low you'd like the appliqué to rest. For extra stability, consider placing a large piece of tear-away stabilizer under the skirt front fabric behind the appliqué area. If the skirt has a built-in lining, make sure not to sew through it.

2. Pin the appliqué to the skirt.

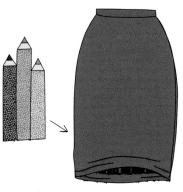

3. Starting at the raw hem edge, topstitch all the way around the appliqué edge, using your preferred finishing stitch. I chose a zigzag.

Tip

I chose a thread color that matches the skirt color, but you could use a nice contrasting thread for more visual interest.

4. Stitch in-the-ditch along either side of rectangle B1 for added definition and stability. If you used tear-away stabilizer on the inside of your skirt, remove it now.

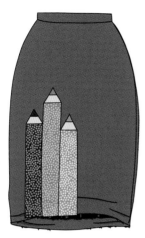

Ta-Dah!

See? You no longer need to fret about your natural-born allergies toward pencil-pushing corporate clothing, because this new addition has sleek, modern, and fun written all over it.

5. Iron the appliqué flat. Trim the bottom appliqué edge to align it with the skirt's raw edge.

6. Turn up and iron the entire hem, incorporating the appliqué bottom edge into the fold.

7. Follow your pattern instructions for finishing the hem, or copy the original store-bought hem, or use your own method. Make sure the raw appliqué edges at the bottom are cleanly finished or folded under.

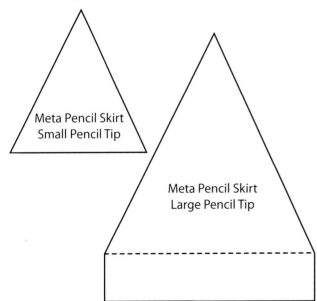

Meta Pencil Skirt
Small Pencil Tip

Meta Pencil Skirt
Large Pencil Tip

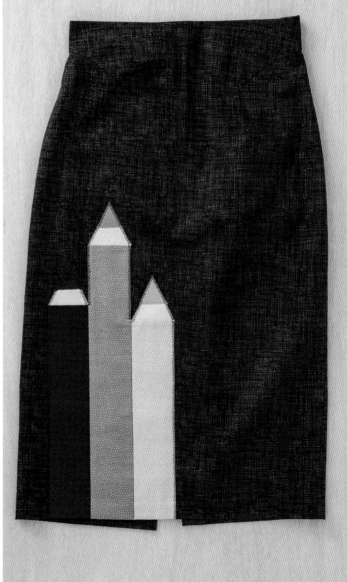

Teacher Tool Belt

Finished size: 20″ × 11½″ without ties

A big part of a schoolteacher's arsenal is the possession and distribution of stickers. Not gonna lie—a big part of my paying attention in class was the very pointed potential of receiving said stickers. It was so much my goal that I practiced my trumpet playing obsessively (you're welcome, Mom and Dad), just so I could earn one of those scratch-n-sniff stickers my fifth-grade band teacher would give out in class. Pizza and peppermint—not a tasty combo in reality, but in sticker form, I'd take them together without hesitation. Fast-forward 30-mumble years: One of my kids' teachers offhandedly remarked that she wished she had a reliable way to have her classroom stickers on hand, because not every outfit she wore had pockets. A light went on in my head as I found the perfect way to perpetuate my unruly obsession with sticker earning to the next generation. And so, the teacher tool belt was born.

fun facts

It's fitting that this project is basically a set of small baglike attachments, because guess what … that's what the definition of pocket *is—or was before pockets began being incorporated into clothing construction. Much like the Scottish sporran, it shares the same Latin root word of* bursa, *or* purse. *If you happen to be either a pocket mouse or a pocket gopher, none of this would matter, because you'd store your stickers in your cheeks and call it a day.*

What You'll Need

- **Pencil tip patterns** (page 30)

- **Pencil color fabrics:** 18 unique fabrics

- **Tan fabric:** for 18 large triangles

  Cut 1 strip 2″ × 27″.

- **Black fabric:** for 18 small triangles

  Cut 1 strip 1″ × 16″.

- **Charcoal fabric:** for front panel and waistband tie binding

  Cut 1 piece 18½″ × 21″.

  Cut 1 strip 2½″ wide × preferred length.

- **Samarra's Fireworks fabric:** for back panel

   Cut 1 piece 18½″ × 21″.

- **Paper-backed fusible webbing:** for triangles

  Cut 1 strip 2″ × 27″.

  Cut 1 strip 1″ × 16″.

It's Go Time!

Seam allowances are ½″ for this project.

1. Decide on the order of colors for your pencils. Note that the pencils are identified alphabetically, starting with A on the left and ending with R on the right. Cut them as follows:

A, F, K, P: each 2″ × 8″

B, G, L, Q: each 2″ × 8¾″

C, H, M, R: each 2″ × 7½″

D, I, N: each 2″ × 7¼″

E, J, O: each 2″ × 8½″

2. Iron paper-backed fusible webbing to the tan and black fabrics. You can cut free-form wonky triangles for your pencil tips like I did, or if you prefer a more unified look, use the Pencil Tip patterns (page 30). Cut out 18 Large Pencil Tip triangles from the tan fabric and 18 Small Pencil Tip triangles from the black fabric.

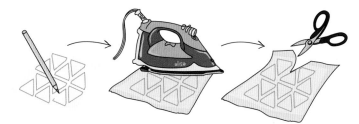

3. Remove the backing from a black small triangle and iron it to the top point of a large triangle, fusing it in place. Repeat this step for a total of 18 pencil tips.

4. Sew a pencil tip to the top of rectangle A. Note that the rectangle is wider to accommodate the pencil seam allowance; so, the pencil tip should be centered horizontally atop the rectangle, ½″ in from each side.

5. Repeat Step 4 to create pencils B through R.

All Together Now

1. Arrange the 18 pencils in alphabetical order to create a spectrum effect. (For a different look, mix them up!) Align the pencils along the bottom. Sew together, right sides facing each other.

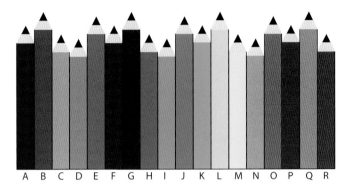

A B C D E F G H I J K L M N O P Q R

2. Iron the allowances flat. Shorter pencil allowances will fold toward their taller neighboring pencils. Be sure to also fold under and iron the ½″ seam allowance on the outer edges of pencils A and R.

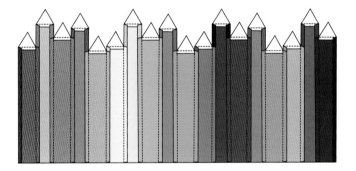

3. Lay the charcoal fabric face-up on a flat surface with a 21″ side closest to you. Fold the bottom edge upward so it overlaps 6½″. This will become the pocket area. Iron along the fold.

4. Open the panel flat again. Align the bottom edge of the pencil appliqué along this creased fold line, centering it horizontally. Pin in place.

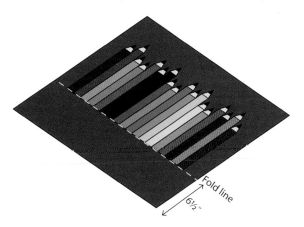

5. Using a small zigzag stitch, sew around the outermost edge of the entire appliqué. I also outlined each of my pencils and pencil leads with this same stitching.

6. Place the front panel and back panels together face to face. Sew the bottom and both sides, leaving the top open.

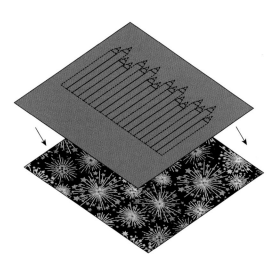

7. Trim off excess fabric at the corners, turn it right side out, and iron flat.

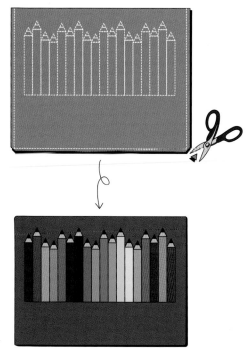

8. Fold the bottom edge upward again so it now measures 6″; pin in place.

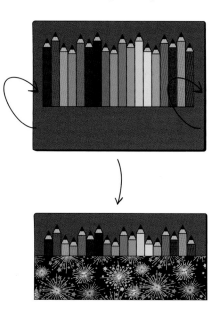

9. For a finished look, topstitch ¼″ from the edge of the panel down the left side, around the bottom, and up the right side. I topstitched another row ½″ in from the edge for added detail and durability.

Almost Done!

1. To make 3 evenly divided pockets, topstitch a line between pencils F and G and another line between pencils L and M. Backstitch along the top of each of these 2 lines to reinforce the pocket openings more.

Tip

You can make pockets of varying widths, including some narrow enough for real pencils and pens to fit in snugly.

2. Attach the waistband tie binding like you would quilt binding (The Ties That Bind, page 121). Begin by folding the 2½″-wide strip (by any custom length desired) in half; press. You can also use premade bias binding if you prefer.

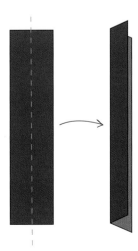

3. Find the center points of the binding tie and the finished tool belt panel, and mark with a pin. Lay the folded binding strip along the top panel edge, aligning its raw edges with the edge of the panel and aligning the center point pins. Pin in place.

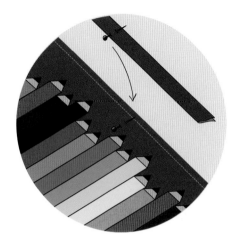

Tip

Why stop at just pockets when, with a bit more binding, you can trick out your tool belt with some handy-dandy carabiners and key loops? I got keys that jingle jangle jingle! If you would like to add these to the top of your tool belt, pin them in place along the top panel edge after Step 1.

4. Using a ¼″ allowance, attach the binding to the panel, making sure not to sew past either end of the panel.

5. The remaining overhanging binding will serve as the waistband ties. Turn the folded edge of the binding to the back of the panel to form the bound edge of the panel with ties on each side. Turn in the tie ends so that the raw edges are hidden. Pin in place.

6. Starting at one tie end, topstitch along the entire length of the waistband tie, over the panel area, and finishing at the other end of the waistband tie. Iron flat.

Small Pencil Tip

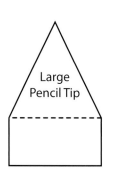

Large Pencil Tip

Ta-Dah!

Time to tie on this tool belt and do a celebratory dance, because you've just completed the perfect year-end teacher-appreciation gift! For that, I give you an A+ sticker. Sure, this belt's great for carrying an array of small classroom supplies, but you know what the sticker-obsessed among us are hoping for!

Lighthouse Dress

Finished dress/bust sizes: Small (34″–35″),
Medium (36″–38″), and Large (39″–41″)

It goes without saying that you're a brick house and you've got it going on (insert self-celebrating air snaps). You're also a beacon, a ray of happiness and light, the steadfast sign in a midnight storm that all will be okay. You're brilliant. And because you're brilliant, you deserve a happy, modern, stately dress that flatters your figure and allows you to have dessert—without giving you the feeling that you wore body-length sausage encasings to dinner. Plus, hello! A dress with pockets?! Say no more.

fun facts

Ever felt like life would be better if you knew just a few more lighthouse-related facts? Yeah, me too. So let's shed some light on the topic now.

- *The tallest traditional-style lighthouse in the world is thought to be the Île Vierge lighthouse in France; the title in the United States goes to North Carolina's Cape Hatteras lighthouse.*

- *Fewer than 700 lighthouses are left in the United States. About 390 of them stand majestically over on the East Coast, while the West Coast has around 94. And who knew Michigan was so crazy needy of the things? It has more than 120 lighthouse specimens within its mitten-grabbing state lines.*

- *Aside from lighthouses being just plain pretty to look at, their daymark patterns are intentionally bold and graphic for easy spotting by mariners in the daytime.*

Look who's bursting with knowledge now, you brightest light in the room, you!

What You'll Need

Yardages are based on 44"–45"-wide fabric.

- **Lighthouse Dress patterns** (pullout pages P1 and P2)

  Refer to Cutting Instructions (below) and pattern layouts (at right) for pieces A, B, C, D, E, and pocket linings.

- **Pale blue fabric:** $1\frac{7}{8}$ yards for pieces A, C, E, and pocket linings

- **Royal blue fabric:** $2\frac{1}{3}$ yards for pieces B and D

- **Lining fabric:** $2\frac{7}{8}$ yards

- **Black fabric:** $\frac{1}{4}$ yard for pockets

  Cut 3 rectangles 6" × 7½" each.

- **Red fabric:** $\frac{1}{8}$ yard for straps

  Cut 4 rectangles 3¾" × 13" each.

- **Red buttons (optional):** 2 buttons 1" diameter or larger for straps

Cutting Instructions

1. Make sure your pattern pullout is free of creases. Trace patterns A, B, C, D, and E for your size (small, medium, or large) onto tissue paper.

2. Fold the pale blue fabric in half widthwise, and use tissue patterns to cut out pieces A, C, and E. Be sure to align the grain lines on the patterns with the straight grain of the fabric. You will be cutting the front and the back at the same time. Refer to the pattern layouts below.

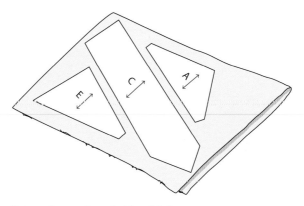

Pattern layout for pale blue fabric

3. Mark the front and back pieces in the seam allowances. You don't want to get them mixed up!

4. Repeat Steps 2 and 3 using the royal blue fabric and patterns B and D.

Pattern layout for royal blue fabric

Tip

Add ⅜" to the side seams to make 1" seam allowances.

This gives you some extra fabric for tweaking the fit.

5. Using the remaining pieces of pale blue fabric, cut out 3 pocket linings 6" × 7½" each.

It's Go Time!

Seam allowances are ⅝″ for this project.

1. Sew all front pieces A, B, C, D and E together to create a complete dress front panel (B to A, C to B, D to C, and E to D).

2. Repeat Step 1 with back pieces A, B, C, D, and E to create complete dress back panel.

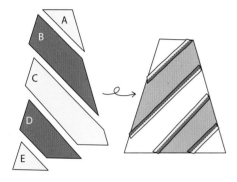

> **Tip**
>
> This is an easy dress to shorten into more of a tunic length. After assembling the main pieces, just cut off to a length that suits you. But don't forget to leave enough fabric for the hem!

3. Press all seams open. Press the front and back panels flat, being careful not to stretch them out of shape.

4. Topstitch ⅛″ on both sides of each seam to create a nice finished look.

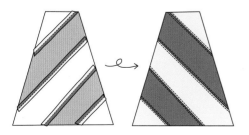

> **Tip**
>
> We will be lining this dress, but if you'd rather skip that, consider using French seams throughout your project; it's a nice way to finish off raw edges.

5. Fold the lining fabric in half widthwise. Using the completed front dress panel as a pattern, cut out the lining. You will be cutting the front and back linings at the same time. Set aside.

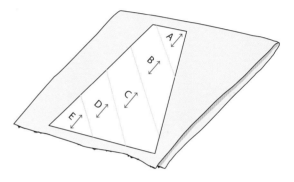

> **Tip**
>
> If you're using the largest size pattern, there'll be a place at the very bottom of the lining where you'll run out of fabric width. No problem—just piece an extra bit of fabric onto the side before cutting. No one will ever know!

> **Tip**
>
> Before cutting the lining, consider folding the dress pattern in half vertically at the center. This will ensure that both sides are symmetrical. Make adjustments as needed.

6. Place 2 of the red fabric rectangles face to face. Stitch them together, starting on one long side, continuing around a short side, and going up the other long side. Leave one short end open. I chose to cut and sew the short end to look like the V-cut of a ribbon end. Do this or leave it with a straight seam.

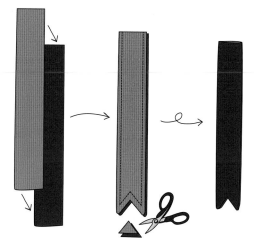

7. Trim off excess fabric at the corners and snip into the allowance if making a V-cut, so the fabric sits flat.

8. Turn the rectangle right side out and iron flat.

9. Repeat Steps 6–8 with the second set of red fabric rectangles. Set aside.

All Together Now

1. Pin the front and back dress panels face to face and sew the side seams together. I stopped mine 9″ from the neckline to allow for the arm opening; adjust yours according to your body measurements.

2. Press the seams open.

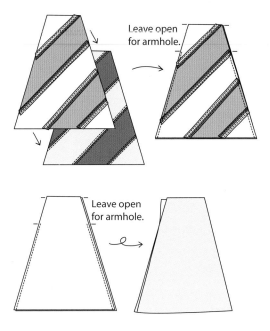

Leave open for armhole.

Leave open for armhole.

3. Repeat Steps 1 and 2 with the lining panels.

4. Turn the lining right side out. Pin each red strap in place to the front lining panel.

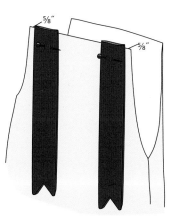

⅝″
⅝″

5. Leave the outer dress wrong side out. Slide the lining (with straps attached) inside the outer dress so that the right side of the lining and the right side of the outer dress are facing one another.

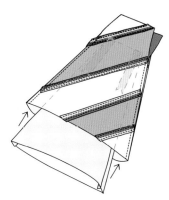

6. Pin the outer dress and lining together at the neckline and the arm openings, making sure that all raw edges are aligned. Sew a continuous seam along the pinned edges, incorporating the straps and pivoting at the side seams.

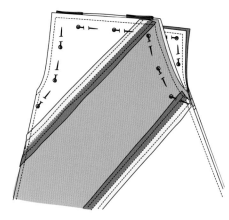

7. Turn the dress right side out so that the wrong sides of the outer dress and lining are facing each other. Iron the neck and armhole seams flat.

8. Smooth out the bottom raw edge of both the outer and lining panels. Turn the bottom edges of both the outer panel and the lining toward the inside, between the panels, at the desired hem length. The hem should be about 1″ in depth. Pin the panels together at the bottom; topstitch closed.

9. Try on the dress to determine where bust darts are needed—you may not want or need them at all. Note that the darts should be short enough to not obstruct the top patch pocket. Mine are each about 1½″ long.

Remember that the dress front has the straps attached.

10. Fold and pin both the outer dress and the lining together to create each dart. With the fold on the lining side, sew to secure the darts in place.

Almost Done!

1. Place a black rectangle 6″ × 7½″ and a pale blue rectangle 6″ × 7½″ face to face. Sew all the way around, leaving a 1″ opening.

2. Cut off excess fabric at the corners. Turn it right side out and fold in the seam allowances of the opening. Iron flat.

3. Repeat Steps 1 and 2 for the remaining 2 pairs of rectangles. These are the dress patch pockets.

4. Place the finished pockets in a column on the front dress panel, so the topmost one is a breast pocket and the remaining two are at hip height. Place pockets with the 1″ opening at the bottom. (The opening will be stitched closed in Step 5.)

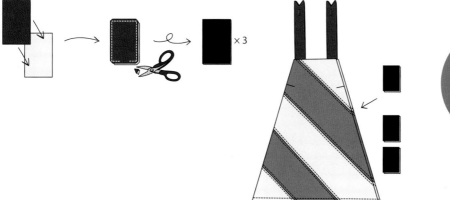

5. Pin and topstitch around the sides and bottom of each rectangle, securing them to the dress. Reinforce each pocket opening by backstitching on the top left and top right.

6. Try on the dress and adjust the back of the straps to a custom fit. I made 2 buttonholes and sewed on coordinating red buttons for my dress. Another option is to topstitch the straps directly onto the top back neckline edge of the dress.

Tip

I placed my patch pockets on the left side of my dress, but if you prefer the right side, move your pockets to that side and follow the assembly instructions above.

Ta-Dah!

Mission accomplished! Dress complete. Look out, sailors! Shine bright in your new frock! It's bold, modern, and fun, just like you. And hey, if you find yourself in a pinch next Halloween, throw this number on, add a headlamp, and call yourself perfectly decked out for any last-minute costume parties! Double-duty! Win-win!

Front of dress

Back of dress

The Bees Knees & Knee-High-to-a-Grasshopper Patches

Finished size: 4¾″ × 4¾″

Know what bugs me? That the knees of kids' pants wear out long before the rest of the pants. Sure, it's probably part of a greater ploy by clothing manufacturers to get us to toss and buy more, but that wasteful option doesn't fly with this mama. Because I refuse to throw them out before their time and I know a person can only own so many cut-offs before an intervention is necessary, I created a couple of bug-buddy patch options that will help take the sting out of inevitable wear-and-tear. Ladies and gentlemen, I present you with The Bee's Knees patch and Knee-High-to-a-Grasshopper patch. Let's get buzzy, people!

fun facts

Thought you weren't being watched in your back garden? Turns out honey-bees can recognize your face. Yes, you read that right. They do something called "configural processing," which means they take all your distinct facial features and mash them all together to make out your entire face. As for grass-hoppers, with their two compound eyes and three simple eyes (imagine what amazing tiny sunglasses they'd have to wear to shield all that), we can bet that these creatures are watching us as well.… But don't let that bug you out or anything.

What You'll Need

Materials and instructions are for making one patch.

Patch patterns (pages 45 and 46) • ***Paper-backed fusible webbing*** • ***Template paper***

Bee's Knees Patch:

- ***Black fabric:*** for body and eyes

- ***White fabric:*** for wings, eyes, and mouth

- ***Yellow fabric:*** for body

- ***Gray patterned fabric:*** for patch front

  Cut 1 square 6″ × 6″.

- ***Black denim fabric:*** for lining

  Cut 1 square 6″ × 6″.

Knee-High-to-a-Grasshopper Patch:

- ***Black fabric:*** for eyes

- ***White fabric:*** for eyes and mouth

- ***Light green fabric:*** for body

- ***Dark green fabric:*** for body

- ***Black patterned fabric:*** for patch front

  Cut 1 square 6″ × 6″.

- ***Black denim fabric:*** for lining

  Cut 1 square 6″ × 6″.

Tip This is a great opportunity to use up some of your seemingly useless scraps. Dig around your fabric supply, mix and match some of those off-cuts, and put them to good use!

My patterns will make 4¾″ × 4¾″ square patches—you can make yours larger or smaller.

It's Go Time!

Seam allowances are ½″ for this project.

1. Using a piece of paper-backed fusible webbing, trace over each pattern piece. Follow the pattern instructions for tracing some pieces in reverse. Trace all the pieces close together and group them by fabric color to minimize paper and fabric waste.

2. Take the grouped tracings of the pattern pieces and iron them onto the wrong side of their corresponding fabrics so each piece is fully fused.

3. Cut out all pieces along the traced lines. Set aside.

4. Trace the patch front/lining pattern onto template paper and cut out. Use the template to cut the patch front and patch lining from the 6″ × 6″ fabric squares.

All Together Now

1. Working directly on the ironing board and using the patch front squares as the background, begin building each bug buddy, making sure to pull off the paper backing from each piece first.

2. For both patch versions, the eye-building treatment is the same: Center each little black circle onto each white circle.

3. Follow the diagrams to build each creature, adjusting and aligning all the pieces until you have them all in place and to your liking.

4. With extra care, use the tip of your hot iron to slowly and systematically tack the center points of each piece in place, starting with the lowest pieces and working your way up. This may take a bit of juggling, but it's well worth it, because it will ensure that everything stays where you want it.

> **Tip** If your regular iron is just too much of a monolith to handle your tiny appliqué pieces, consider investing in a small tacking iron. These little irons are handy and especially good for any dapper mice you might know who like to iron their own dress shirts. (I look out for all creatures.) Another route is to use your standard iron in one hand and a heat-resistant stylus in the other to hold each piece in place. It's another cost-effective way to stop piece shifting while simultaneously making ironing a spectator sport.

5. When all the pieces are in place, iron the entire patch flat on both sides to fuse everything in place.

Almost Done

1. Topstitch around all appliqué edges for added durability. I did this step by hand with heavy-duty thread.

2. Using white embroidery thread, stitch highlights on the buggy eyes to make them twinkle.

3. Place the appliquéd patch front and the lining square face to face; pin together.

> **Tip** For added body, consider sandwiching batting between the patch front and the denim lining, or perhaps add fusible interfacing. If you choose to do so, cut out a piece of batting or interfacing the same size as the patch front. Add batting to the top or bottom of your face-to-face fabrics. Fuse interfacing to either the patch front or the denim lining.

4. Straight stitch all the way around the square, making smooth curves at the corners and leaving a 1½″ opening on one side.

5. Cut off excess corner fabric and snip into the seam allowance around curves, so the fabric sits flat once it's right side out.

6. Turn the finished buggy bug patch right side out and hand sew the opening shut. Iron flat.

7. Stitch the finished patches to the knees of your kiddo's pants.

> **Tip** These patches also make great pockets. So add them to shirts, jackets, back pockets, or wherever you like! If you're making a pair of grasshopper patches, remember to reverse the second one so the two grasshoppers are facing each other.

Ta-Dah!

Say bye-bye to those pesky holes and rips and hello to fly new pants. These new bug buddies are sure to put an extra spring in the step of the kids who wear them.

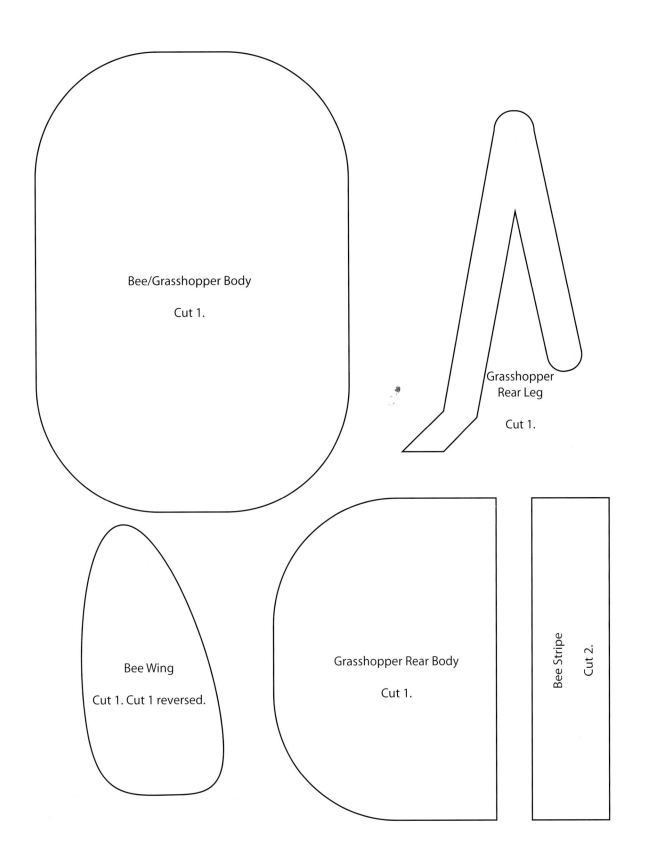

Bee/Grasshopper Body

Cut 1.

Grasshopper
Rear Leg

Cut 1.

Bee Wing

Cut 1. Cut 1 reversed.

Grasshopper Rear Body

Cut 1.

Bee Stripe

Cut 2.

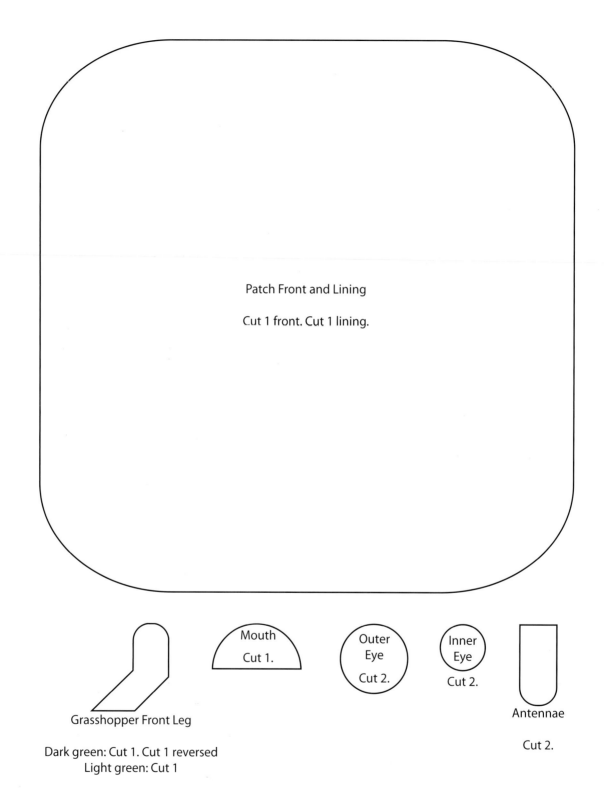

Patch Front and Lining

Cut 1 front. Cut 1 lining.

Mouth
Cut 1.

Outer
Eye
Cut 2.

Inner
Eye
Cut 2.

Grasshopper Front Leg

Dark green: Cut 1. Cut 1 reversed
Light green: Cut 1

Antennae

Cut 2.

Home Decor

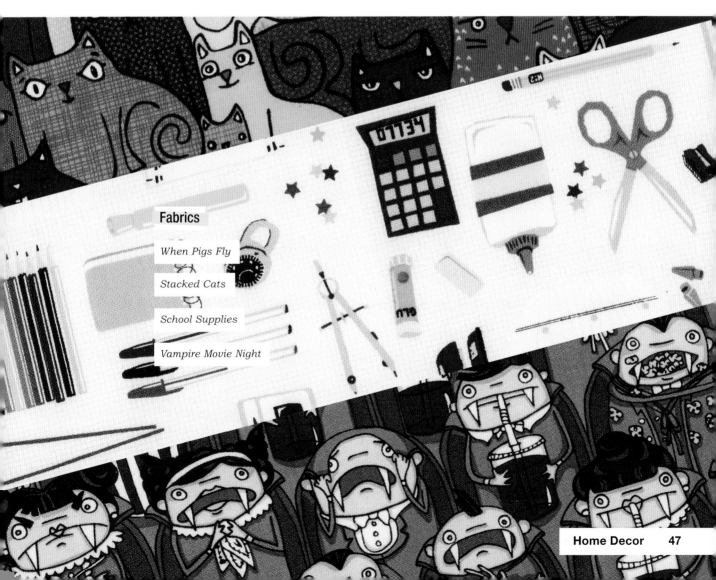

Fabrics

When Pigs Fly

Stacked Cats

School Supplies

Vampire Movie Night

Typewriter Tissue Box Cover

Finished size: fits standard tissue box 9″ long × 4¾″ wide × 4¼″ high

If you're anything like me, you find tissue boxes downright hideous to look at; yet they are a component to just about every room in my house. In an attempt to jazz them up, I've sought covers on the open market but have only found fun options made to fit small pixie-portioned boxes of tissues—for social and sometimes weekend sneezers, I can only presume. You too? Not to worry, fellow big box tissue buyers! We can make this typewriter cover. Not only will it hide The Ugly, but it will also magically transforms each two-ply sheet of masterful absorbency into the pretend pages of that Great American Novel you've been planning to write. Perhaps it's a mystery novel about the boogey man. Go get 'em, Agatha Chri-sneeze.

fun facts

Ever tried to stop a sneeze? It's basically impossible to do, because it's an automatic reflex. That's proof positive that it's never a good thing to sneeze and drive. It's also never a good idea to drive as fast as a sneeze travels, unless you're a glutton for speeding tickets. Sneezes travel upward of 100 miles per hour. Know what else? The nerve reflexes that initiate sneezing actually rest while you sleep (kinda creepy, no?), which is why we don't sneeze in our sleep. Which reminds me, don't drive in your sleep either.

What You'll Need

- **Typewriter Tissue Box Cover patterns** (pullout pages P1 and P2)

- **Turquoise fabric:** 1 fat quarter or ½ yard for typewriter body

  Cut 1 rectangle 15¾″ × 20″.

- **White lining fabric:** 1 fat quarter or ½ yard for body lining

  Cut 1 rectangle 15¾″ × 20″.

- **Black fabric:** ¼ yard for keyboard background (E), typewriter roller (F), and 2 small roller knobs (H)

- **Medium gray fabric:** for 2 large roller knobs (G) and 1 key (C)

- **White / pale gray polka-dot fabric:** for carriage return lever (I)

- **White fabric:** for 19 typewriter keys (A) and 1 space bar (D)

- **Red fabric:** for 1 red key (B)

- **Fusible interfacing:** ½ yard of 15″-wide interfacing for side panels and carriage return lever

  Cut 2 squares 5¼″ × 5¼″.

  Cut 2 rectangles 5¼″ × 9½″.

- **Paper-backed fusible webbing:** ¼ yard for roller, keyboard background, and typewriter keys

- **Template paper**

It's Go Time!

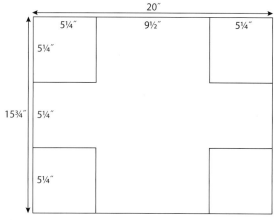

Typewriter body and lining pattern measurements

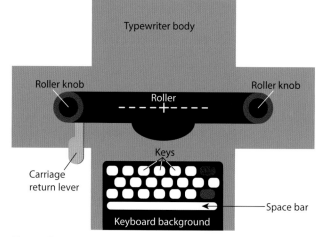

Typewriter assembly

1. Cut out the typewriter body and lining pieces, using the pattern measurements as your guide. My tissue box measures 9″ long × 4¾″ wide × 4¼″ tall, and its opening is 5½″ long. If your tissue box is a different measurement, adjust the body fabric measurements by adding ½″ to the original box length and width and 1″ to the height. You will need to adjust the fusible interfacing measurements as well. All appliqué embellishments can be used at the pattern size with just a slight positioning adjustment, if needed, to give you a custom fit.

2. Place the typewriter body fabric wrong side up on the ironing board and position the 2 squares and 2 rectangles of fusible interfacing, fusible side down, to the sides. Iron in place. Set aside.

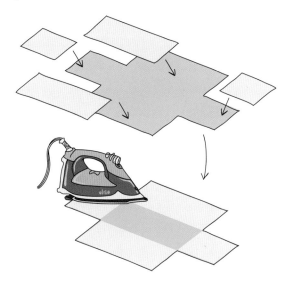

3. Trace the pattern for the keyboard background (pattern E) onto template paper. Cut out from black fabric and fusible webbing. Set the fusible webbing aside.

4. Trace all typewriter keyboard shapes (patterns A, B, C, and D) onto the fusible webbing paper, leaving space between each shape. Loosely cut out around each traced shape and iron them to the back of their corresponding fabrics.

5. Cut out all the fused shapes along the drawn lines.

6. Remove the paper backing from the typewriter keys (A, B, C, D) and arrange them on the black keyboard background (no webbing is applied to this piece yet). After they are positioned as shown in the keyboard assembly diagram, iron them in place.

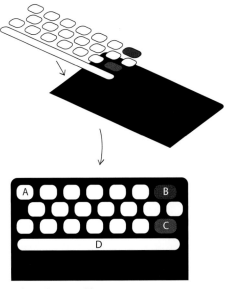

Keyboard assembly

7. For added durability, topstitch around all the key edges. I hand stitched these using matching thread for each key.

8. Iron fusible webbing to the back of the finished main keyboard background (E). Set aside.

9. Trace the roller knob shapes (patterns H and G) onto fusible webbing. Loosely cut around each shape. Iron the shapes to the back of their corresponding fabrics.

10. Cut out fused roller knob shapes H and G.

11. Remove the backing from one shape H and center it on one shape G. Iron in place. Repeat to make 2 roller knobs. Set aside.

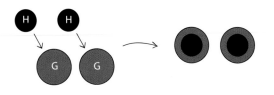

12. Trace the carriage return lever (pattern I) onto template paper. Use the template on a folded piece of the polka-dot fabric and cut 2 mirror image shapes. Cut 1 shape in fusible stabilizer. Sandwich the 2 pieces of fabric face to face. Place the fusible stabilizer on top and pin all 3 layers together.

13. Using a ¼″ seam allowance, stitch around the lever, leaving the narrow end open. Turn right side out and iron flat.

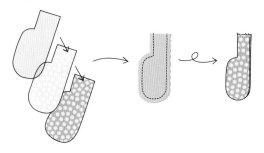

All Together Now

1. With the typewriter body fabric placed right side up on a flat surface and using the typewriter assembly diagram (page 50) as a guide, lay the finished keyboard in place. Align it in the center horizontally, with its bottom raw edge flush to the bottom edge of the typewriter fabric. Iron in place.

2. Topstitch around the sides and top of the finished keyboard, leaving the bottom edge unstitched.

3. Trace the typewriter roller pattern (F) onto the fusible webbing and iron it to the back of the black fabric.

4. Cut out the typewriter roller and remove the backing. Using the typewriter assembly diagram (page 50) as a guide, position the roller in the center of the typewriter body.

5. Remove the backings from the 2 roller knobs. Position them so they are aligned as shown in the roller assembly diagram. Gently lift up the left circle / roller end just enough to tuck under ½″ of the raw-edged end of the carriage return lever.

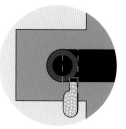

Roller assembly

6. Iron all shapes in place. *A*

7. Use black thread to topstitch around the black roller edges and the black inner roller knob circles.

8. Use gray thread to topstitch around the outer roller knob circles.

9. Place the typewriter body fabric and lining fabric face to face, matching all edges. Pin together.

10. Mark the center line for the tissue box opening on the back of the typewriter body, as shown on the typewriter roller pattern. If your box opening length is not the same as on the pattern, adjust accordingly, making sure to keep it centered. I marked mine at 5½″ long. *B*

11. Sew a rounded-corner rectangle ¼″ away from the line all the way around. *C*

12. Slit the centered line open through all the layers of fabric (outer, lining, and appliqué). At each corner of the newly sewn rectangle, snip into the seam allowance at a 45° angle, making sure not to cut your stitching.

13. Turn everything right side out. Iron the top opening flat and topstitch ⅛″ around it to keep it secure. The lining and outer cover are now attached, wrong sides facing, and ready for hemming.

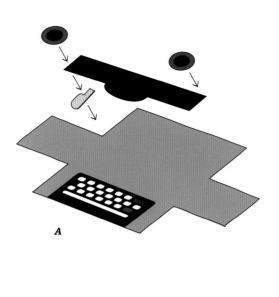

A

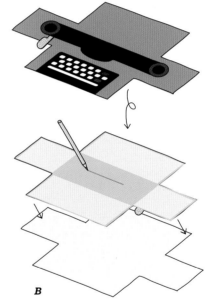

B

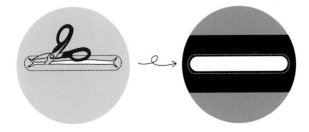

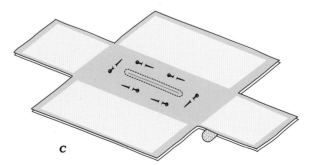

C

Almost Done!

1. Using a ¼″ allowance, sew the lining together, with right sides facing. To do this, take neighboring edges of the side panels and pin them together. Sew from edge to edge. Press seams open. Repeat with the remaining panel side edges.

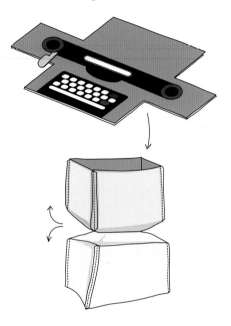

2. Repeat Step 1 with the typewriter body.

3. The bottom raw edge is the only thing left to sew. To ensure that it is hemmed at the correct length, place the lining, wrong side out, over your tissue box. Work your way around the box, folding up the lining hem so that it is even with the bottom of the box. Pin in place.

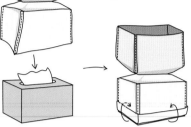

4. Remove the cover and iron the lining hem flat, taking out the pins as you press.

5. Place the typewriter body, wrong side out, over the tissue box. Again, work your way around the box, folding up the lower edge so that it is even with the bottom of the box. Pin in place.

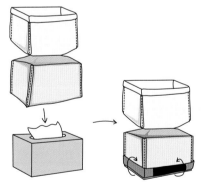

6. Remove the cover from the tissue box. Iron the folded hem of the typewriter body flat, taking out the pins as you press. Align the folded edges of the lining and typewriter body; pin together. Topstitch ¼″ from the edge.

Ta-Dah!

That's all she wrote, folks! Your typewriter tissue box cover is ready for action, uniting your retro love of prose with sniffly love for your nose.

Red Stapler Pillow

Finished size: 14″ × 14″

Staplers are beautiful things. They are used for furniture manufacturing, carpet tacking, insulation and electrical wire installation, picture frame manufacturing, stitching in medical fields, and of course home/office use. Who knew one tiny bent piece of metal could afford us with so many options in life? Because something so seemingly mundane does so much for us, it only makes sense to give it a wink and shout-out. Hello, throw pillow. Yes, I know I read your mind on that one. Not to worry, ducklings, we are one here, and we both know a red stapler pillow is the next necessary addition to any self-respecting household. So let's get to it.

fun facts

Swingline. Office Space. Need I say more? If you know the movie, you know all about red Swingline staplers. But did you know that none existed before the movie came out in 1999? A handful were sprayed red at an auto body paint shop for prop use in the movie. When people saw the beautiful specimens twinkling on the big screen, they barraged Swingline with requests for red staplers. In 2002, the company obliged. Since then, all has been right in the land.

What You'll Need

- **Red Stapler patterns** (pullout page P1)

- **Turquoise fabric:** 1 square 15″ × 15″ for pillow front

- **Red fabric:** for stapler body

- **Orange fabric:** for stapler highlights

- **Gray fabric:** for stapler accents

- **Dark print fabric:** for stapler base

- **Samarra's School Supplies fabric:** for pillow back

  Cut 1 square 15″ × 15″.

- **Striped fabric and piping cord (optional):** for piping

- **Metallic silver thread:** for accents

- **Paper-backed fusible webbing**

- **Pillow insert:** 14″ × 14″

It's Go Time

Seam allowances are ½″ for this project.

1. Trace all pattern pieces onto paper-backed fusible webbing, leaving extra paper around each piece. Note that the patterns are in reverse so that the pieces will be oriented correctly for fusing (Steps 4 and 5). Refer to the stapler assembly diagram below as a cutting guide.

2. Iron each loosely cut piece to the back of its corresponding fabric; fuse in place.

3. Cut out all stapler pieces along the pencil lines, cutting through the paper and fabric layers.

4. Place the pillow background fabric flat on the ironing board, and position all stapler pieces into the center area of the fabric square, using the pattern as your guide.

5. Iron to fuse all the layers together. Tack first, if necessary, to ensure that the pieces don't shift before they're permanently secured.

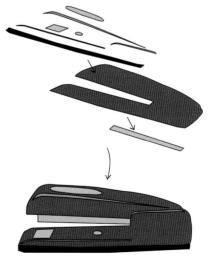

Stapler assembly

All Together Now

1. Use metallic silver embroidery thread to hand embroider the remaining stapler accents.

Tip

If you don't feel embroidery is your strong suit, but you're a boss at cutting and ironing, consider cutting these last remaining stapler details out of additional fabric with paper-backed fusible and ironing them into place.

2. Topstitch around all raw appliqué areas for a finished look. I used a zigzag stitch. You may choose to use a hand-sewn finishing stitch—perhaps blanket, chain, or other fun embroidery stitch.

Almost Done!

Tip

If you want to add more fun to your pillow like I did, add piping or another trim, or, hello, can you go wrong with pom-poms!?! If you like that idea, sandwich them in between the pillow panels as part of Step 1, so you can sew it all together in one shot. Use your own tried-and-true method for joining the piping ends.

1. Place the appliquéd pillow front and back fabric together, face to face, aligning all edges. Pin in place. (Remember, piping is optional here.)

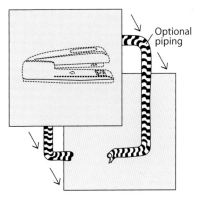

Optional piping

2. Starting along the bottom edge, sew all the way around the pillow cover, leaving a 5″ centered opening on one side for turning the pillow right side out.

3. Trim off excess fabric at the corners, flip the pillow right side out, and iron flat. Slipstitch the opening closed. *A*

4. Insert the pillow form into the cover and hand sew the opening shut. *B*

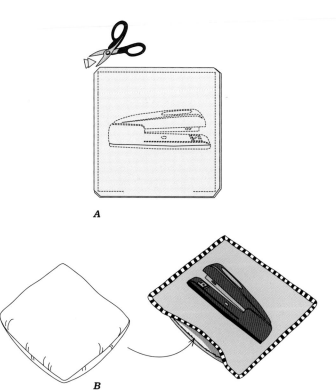

A

B

Ta-Dah!

Mission complete! Yes, this pillow would look great in an office. But because we are fans of the not-so-obvious and unpredictable surprises, let's put this grand new addition on a sofa or bed for unexpected flair. Because there should always be high levels of flair. Flair, flair, everywhere.

Toothy, the Tooth Fairy

Finished size: 8¾″ wide × 10½″ high × 2½″ deep

Gah! You know what I'm sick of? Tooth fairy pillows always being girls—overly frilly girl fairies, carting around lost baby teeth. With two boys, I want more options, more unisex and boy-friendly offerings than are commercially available. So, as I often do, I took matters into my own hands. That's when Toothy, the Tooth Fairy came along. Yes, that's right, with tube socks.…You're welcome.

fun facts

While the tooth fairy reigns supreme in the United States, it's a tooth mouse that gets most of the dental glory across Europe. Mice supposedly have strong teeth, and so this is one rodent characteristic that many humans are willing to covet. Head to parts of Asia, India, and the Middle East and you need a good pitching arm—most traditions there involve throwing a tooth somewhere. Seriously, you're told to throw it every which way: toward the sun, onto or over house rooftops, between the legs, into a fire while making a wish, vertically up into the air as straight as possible to ensure straight teeth. And of course, there's also this universally recognized ritual of ushering in adult teeth—inadvertently swallowing a baby tooth shortly after it falls out. It's far from a planned formal tradition, but it happens everywhere.

What You'll Need

- *Toothy patterns* (pages 71–73)

For tooth body:

- *Ivory fabric:* for upper tooth body and crown

  Cut 1 rectangle 6″ × 22″ (strip A).

  Cut 1 rectangle 5″ × 10″ for tooth crown.

- *Light tan fabric:* for middle of tooth body

  Cut 1 rectangle 3″ × 22″ (strip B).

- *White-on-cream striped fabric:* for lower tooth body

  Cut 2 rectangles 1½″ × 22″ each (strips C and E).

  Cut 1 rectangle 3″ × 22″ (strip G).

- *Red fabric:* for sock stripes

  Cut 2 rectangles 1½″ × 22″ (strips D and F).

For tooth wings and backpack:

- *Yellow fabric:* for wings

  Cut 4 rectangles 7″ × 9″.

- *Orange fabric:* for outer backpack

  Cut 1 rectangle 7″ × 9½″.

- *Matching orange ribbon:* ¾″ wide for backpack

  Cut 2 pieces 9″ long and 1 piece 2″ long.

- *Samarra's Stacked Cats (or Vampire Movie Night) fabric:* for backpack lining

   Cut 1 rectangle 7″ × 9½″.

For Toothy details:

- *White fabric:* for mouth
- *Blue fabric:* for eyes
- *Black fabric:* for eyes
- *Black fabric:* for missing tooth
- *Embroidery thread:* for face and personalized name label
- *Pearl snap closures*
- *Stuffing*
- *Batting*
- *Paper-backed fusible webbing*
- *Beads and sequins (optional)*
- *Template paper*

It's Go Time!

Seam allowances are ½˝ for this project.

1. Attach all rectangular strips (A–G) in alphabetical order. Iron flat, with all seams folding in the same downward direction toward the G piece.

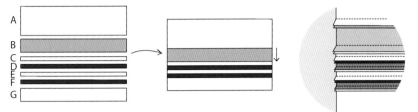

Tip

I chose red fabric for my Toothy's tube sock stripes. Consider changing your stripe colors, especially if you're making multiples and want each one to look unique. Go crazy and customize!

2. Fold the assembled panel in half, right sides together, so it measures 11˝ × 12˝. Make sure that all stripes match across the panel and at the raw edges.

3. Trace the Main Body pattern and the horizontal guideline onto template paper. Pin the body template to the center of your folded panel. Align the dashed line on the pattern with the top of stripe B. The fold will be trimmed off. (You've only kept it here to help align the stripes so the side seams will match up nicely when you sew.)

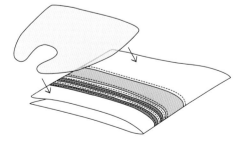

4. Cut out the entire shape, leaving pins in place. Set aside.

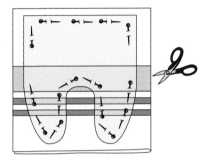

5. Trace the wing pattern onto template paper. Use the template to trace the wing onto the wrong sides of 2 yellow rectangles.

6. Stack 2 yellow rectangles, right sides facing, one with the wing tracing and one without. Place the stacked yellow rectangles on top of a 7˝ × 9˝ piece of batting. Pin together.

7. Sew around the wing, leaving the small straight end open. Snip into the seam allowance all the way around for better curving. Turn the wing right side out. Iron flat.

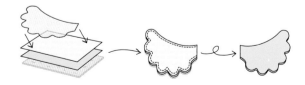

8. Repeat Steps 6 and 7 for the second wing.

> **Tip**
>
> **Here's a place to add some fun, festive embellishments. Adding buttons, beads, or sequins on each wing will make them look extra magical!**

9. Leaving all other pins intact, unpin the sides of the main Toothy body and tuck in the wings to either side, aligning them to sit right above the join of fabrics A and B. Ensure that the wings are symmetrically placed and facing inward, with their raw edges aligned with the body's raw edges. Pin in place. *A*

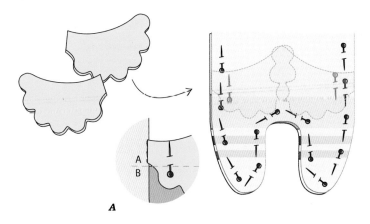

A

10. Remove the template, but keep the stripes on the front and back of the body matched with a few pins. Beginning at the upper right corner of the Toothy body, sew down and around each tube-socked leg and back up the left side, keeping the top edge open and making sure that the wings get sewn in place as you go. Snip into the seam allowance all the way around to make sure all the curves will sit flat. *B*

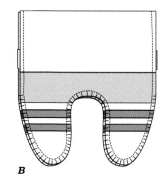

B

11. Turn right side out and iron flat. *C*

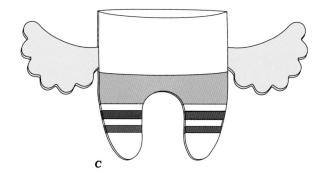

C

All Together Now

1. Trace all the face detail pieces—H (2), I (2), J, and K—onto the fusible webbing paper, leaving extra paper around each piece to cut them all out.

2. Iron each loosely cut detail piece onto its corresponding fabric; fuse in place.

3. Cut out each fused shape along the pencil lines.

4. Remove the paper backing from the 2 black circles H and center them on each blue circle I. Iron and fuse in place. Set aside.

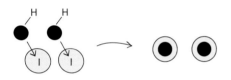

> ## Tip
>
> **If you're giving Toothy as a gift and would like a more personalized feel, consider changing that outer circle eye color to match Toothy's new owner. I chose a blue for mine to match my eldest son's eyes.**

5. Fold piece K in half lengthwise and then in sixths widthwise. Finger-press to create creases in the paper and fabric layers. Mark the grid lightly with pencil on the fabric's right side. This grid is Toothy's toothy grin.

6. Remove the paper backing from "missing tooth" piece J and place it into any preferred grid block within Toothy's grin. Iron it in place.

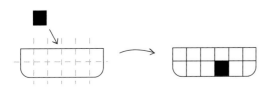

7. Remove the paper backing from the eye circles and the mouth piece. Place them symmetrically on Toothy's face, using the pattern as your positioning guide. Iron and fuse all pieces in place.

8. Use embroidery thread to hand stitch around all appliquéd facial features for a finished look. Complete Toothy's big grin by outlining the 11 remaining pearly whites (plus that one gap tooth) with black embroidery thread, following the grid lines and fabric edges. Use coordinating embroidery thread to chain stitch around each iris and pupil. Use white thread to embroider little highlight spots in Toothy's eyes, making them twinkle even more.

9. Use the Crown pattern to cut out the oval tooth crown piece from 5″ × 10″ ivory rectangle.

Tip

To trick Toothy out even further, consider cutting a matching crown piece from batting. Sandwich it behind your white fabric crown piece and, using white embroidery thread, embroider a star burst or elongated asterisks at its center. I used a split stitch for mine. This makes for a nice added dimensional detail that will make Toothy look even more special.

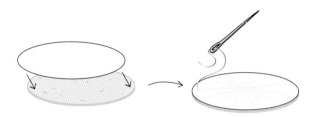

10. Turn the Toothy body inside out and pin the oval top all the way around the open end, making sure it's centered along both horizontal and vertical axes.

11. Once fully pinned, sew the crown to the body, beginning at the center of the body back panel and leaving a 1½″ opening.

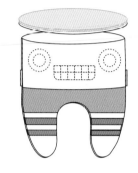

Almost Done!

1. Turn Toothy right side out again and stuff to fill the body cavity. Make sure Toothy's tube-socked legs are stuffed as evenly as the rest of his body. Once he is stuffed to your liking, hand sew the remaining hole closed with a ladder stitch.

2. Starting at the back center area of Toothy's body, pin a 9″ length of ribbon so it loops around to the front, around a wing, and back to the same starting point. Pin in place.

3. Repeat Step 2 with the remaining ribbon and wing.

4. Hand stitch along both edges of each ribbon to secure them to Toothy's body, so they stay put around each wing. Do not worry about the raw ribbon edges; they will all be covered by the backpack itself. Set aside.

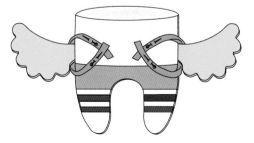

5. Place the 7″ × 9½″ backpack and lining fabrics face to face, and sandwich a piece of same-size batting on the bottom, pinning all 3 layers in place.

6. Starting along a long side, sew all the way around the rectangle, leaving a 1″ opening.

7. Snip into the seam allowance at the corners. Turn right side out. Iron flat.

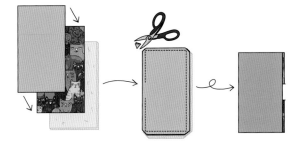

8. Fold the rectangle into thirds, so the bottom 2 sections measure 3¼″ high each and the top section measures 2″ high, using the template as your guide. Note that the 2″ section forms the backpack's top flap.

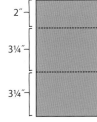

9. Topstitch a straight line across each of the fold lines from Step 8.

10. For a more personalized feel, I hand embroidered the name of Toothy's recipient onto the backpack.

11. Add pearl snap closures to the backpack, following the manufacturer's instructions.

12. Pin the backpack to the back center area of Toothy, covering all raw ribbon ends.

13. Take a 2″-long piece of ribbon and fold it in half to create a loop (**A**). Place this at the center top of your backpack, tucking the raw edges in between the Toothy body and backpack. This loop serves a dual purpose—it will visually look like the backpack handle, while also holding a new toothbrush for your toothless recipient. Make sure to test that your toothbrush handle fits snugly through the loop; adjust the ribbon length accordingly. **B**

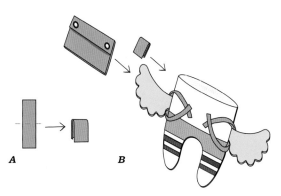

A   B

14. Ladder stitch all the way around the backpack, incorporating in and securing the ribbon loop and closing up the 1″ side seam opening. The backpack side seams are closed with the ladder stitching, but be sure to leave the pocket flap unattached at the sides. Make sure that everything is well attached and flat.

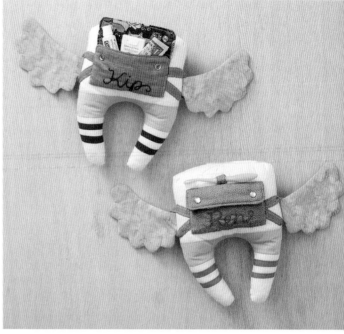

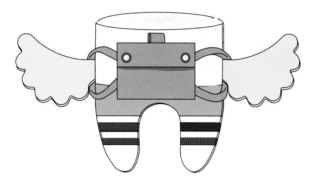

Ta-Dah!

Toothy, the Tooth Fairy, is now polished and ready to receive a brand new loose tooth in his backpack at bedtime from your resident toothless wonder. By morning, with the help of good old-fashioned magic (a.k.a. stealth moves by parental units), the tooth will have been replaced with a sparkly new toothbrush, mini tube of toothpaste, and a pack of floss, 'cause Toothy cares deeply about oral hygiene and likes to show it. Oh yeah, and some cold, hard cash. Don't forget the cold, hard cash.

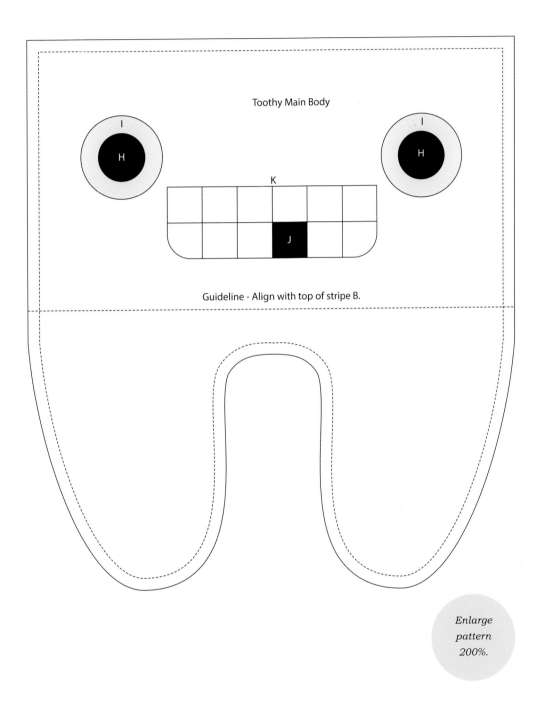

Toothy Main Body

Guideline - Align with top of stripe B.

Enlarge pattern 200%.

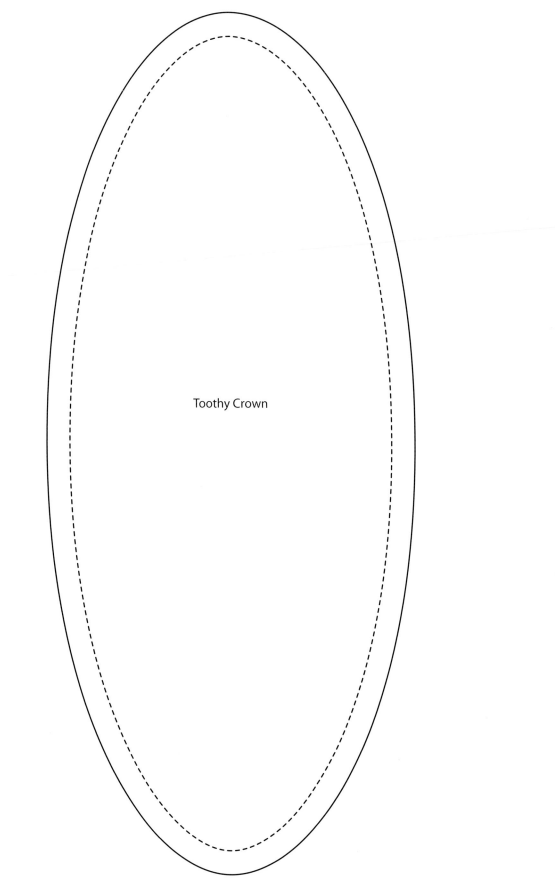

Toothy Crown

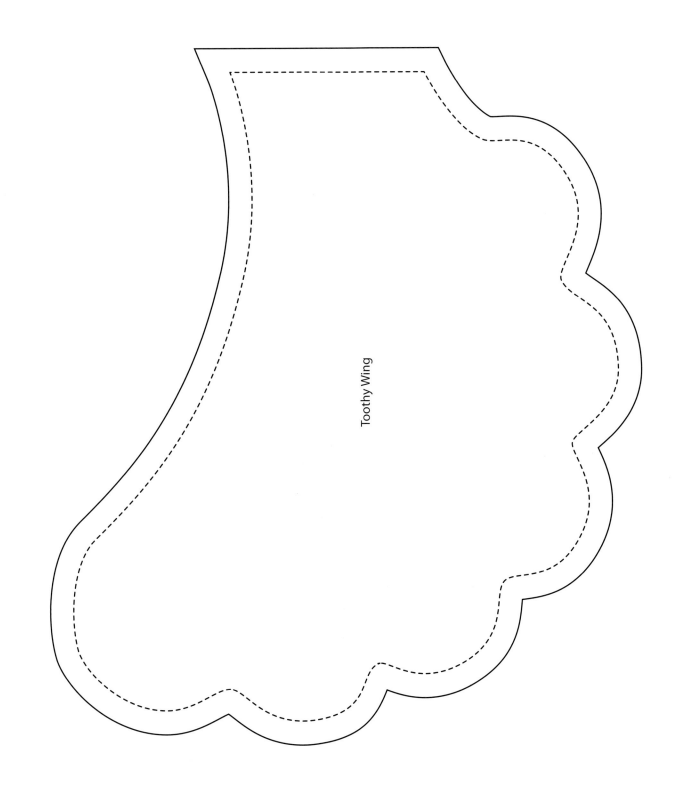

Toothy Wing

Reversible Notepaper Shower Curtain

Finished size: 70″ × 70″

Many of the best brainstorms happen in the shower. It's probably because of the heightened dopamine flow. But maybe it's because you're metamorphosing from stinky to squeaky clean, and your body wants to thank you by giving you uninterrupted time to brainstorm and daydream to your heart's content. Okay, maybe it really is the dopamine. Either way, awesome mental notes can always use awesome notepaper. So let's transform that ho-hum shower curtain into a larger-than-life place for your finest thoughts to reveal themselves.

fun facts

Got some ruled paper? Seems a simple enough question, but there are quite a few different standardized types of ruled paper within the United States and even more variations worldwide. I bet you've heard of some of these before and others not so much: You've got your legal (a.k.a. wide) ruled, college (a.k.a. medium) ruled, narrow ruled, Gregg ruled, Pitman ruled, and manuscript ruled. If we bring graph paper into the mix, there's also quadrille, semi-log, and log-log ruled options. Wait, who ruled what now? So next time someone asks for a sheet of lined paper, feel free to silence the room in nanoseconds by rattling off these options.

What You'll Need

- **Pale gray fabric:** 4½ yards for front

  Cut into 2 lengths 2¼ yards each.

- **Light blue fabric:** 2 yards for lines

  Cut 12 strips 2½″ × 71″ each.

- **Red fabric:** 2 yards for stripes

  Cut 2 strips 2½″ × 71″ each.

- **Samarra's When Pigs Fly fabric:** 4½ yards for lining

   Cut into 2 lengths 2¼ yards each.

- **Curtain grommets:** 16 (I used Dritz curtain grommets in brushed silver finish.)

Tip

Using two yards of red fabric allows you to make the strips in one piece. If you are willing to piece the strips, you can use a lot less fabric.

It's Go Time!

Seam allowances are ½″ for this project unless otherwise noted.

1. Using a 1″ seam allowance, sew the 2 pieces of pale gray fabric together face to face along the selvage edge, making sure the seam is straight. Trim the allowance down to ½″.

2. Iron the allowance flat. With this new seamline running vertically down the center, trim the assembled fabric to 71″ × 71″ square.

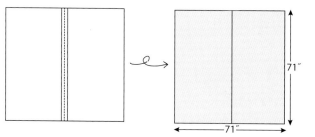

3. Repeat Steps 1 and 2 with the lining fabric. Set aside.

4. Fold a light blue strip in half vertically. Iron flat.

5. Using a ¼″ allowance, sew all the way down this vertical raw edge to create a tube. Turn it right side out and iron flat with the seam at the back of the strip.

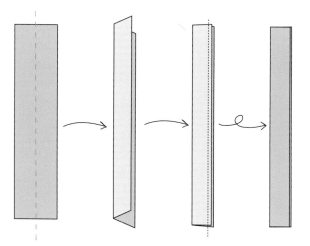

6. Repeat Steps 4 and 5 with the remaining 11 light blue strips and 2 red strips.

7. With the pale gray curtain panel lying flat, pin a light blue strip vertically over the center seam to cover it, aligning the top and bottom raw edges.

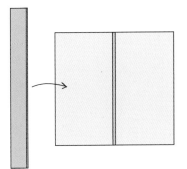

8. Working your way outward from the center vertical stripe, place and pin the remaining blue strips equally spaced and parallel to each other. I placed mine approximately 4″ apart, leaving a 6″ band of pale gray on the leftmost edge and an 9″ band of pale gray on the rightmost edge.

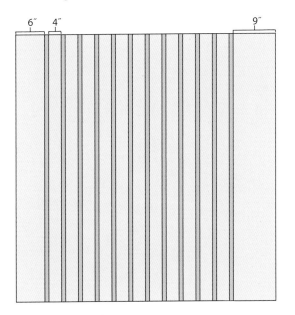

9. Topstitch all blue strips in place.

10. Place a red strip horizontally across the width of the curtain panel, so the strip measures 8½″ down from the topmost edge of the panel. Ensure that the strip aligns with the left and right raw edges. Pin in place.

11. Place and pin the second red strip below the first one, with a spacing of 1½″ in between. Pin in place. Topstitch both red strips in place.

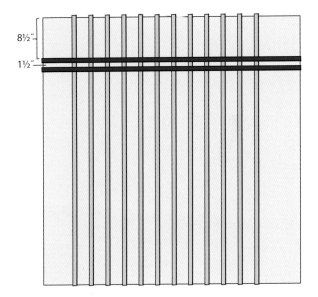

Tip

If you want to personalize your notepaper, consider embroidering or appliquéing text to a few of your lines. It could be the names of everyone in the house or a favorite family phrase or message, such as "Rinse and repeat. And don't forget your feet!"

All Together Now

1. Place the finished front panel face to face with the lining panel, aligning all edges. Pin together. Beginning along the bottom edge, sew all the way around all edges, leaving a 4″ opening at the bottom.

Tip

You may want to have nice right-angle corners on your notepaper curtain, or you may want slightly rounded corners. If you prefer rounded corners, now's the time to draw quarter-circle curves at each corner to act as guidelines when you sew up your seams. If you do use this technique, make sure to snip into your allowance to get smoother curves when you turn the fabric right side out.

2. Trim off excess fabric at the corners and turn the entire curtain right side out. Iron flat.

3. Topstitch around all curtain edges to keep the front panel and lining in place.

Almost Done!

Follow the grommet manufacturer's instructions for grommet attachment to the curtain. For grommet placement, place the center point of the 2 outermost grommets 2¼″ in from the outer edges and 2¼″ down from the top curtain edge. Space the remaining 14 grommets equally between them.

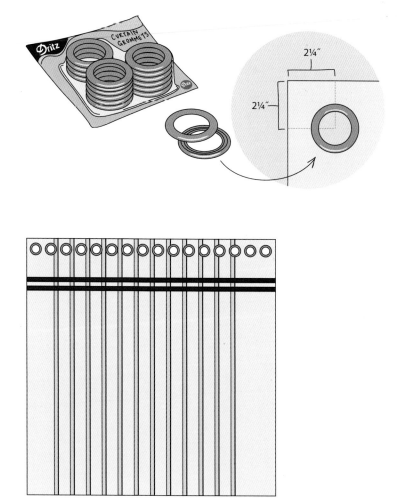

Ta-Dah!

Your reversible notepaper shower curtain is now complete and ready to hang! Add a clear plastic waterproof liner on the inside, and then you'll be able to admire all your handwork. Time to go bathe and brainstorm, you copious note-taker, you!

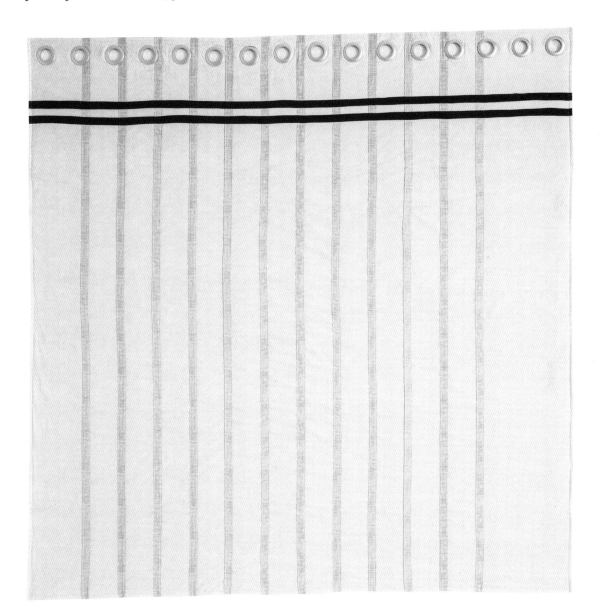

Prehistoric Portrait Painting

Finished size: 20″ × 24″

If your household is anything like mine, there's a whole lot of dinosaur love going on. Maybe I am blissfully delusional, but to me it only makes sense that these venerable creatures who once roamed the Earth be treated to the same majestic levels of prestige and honor that are bestowed upon our country's presidents, educational institution leaders, and any other fancy-schmancy individuals in history. Maybe I've swigged the punch for too long, but I think their existence has merited a portrait be painted of them. I'm talking old-world master levels of tribute here, folks, so let's get cracking before we're all extinct.

fun facts

Before photography, portrait paintings were the only way to record what people looked like, and it was the rare elite who got to take full advantage of this self-aggrandizing opportunity. So, of course, these wealthy folk would often cram in a lot of symbolism to show off, from certain berries to animals to armillary spheres, orbs, scepters, and staffs. A whole lot of visual bragging was going on.

The painters did it, too. They had subtle contests to see who could paint the best-draped fabric behind a subject or who could dexterously portray a foreshortened arm and elbow pose, which could be a perspective nightmare. Portrait painting was such a popular and lucrative venture that some artists opted to focus on the face of the subject and then farm out the rest of the picture to assistants to fill in. What a crafty lot.

What You'll Need

Refer to the color key diagram (page 83) for use of each fabric color.

- **Prehistoric Portrait Painting patterns (in reverse)** (pullout page P2)

- **Olive green fabric (A):** for dinosaur skin

- **Dark green fabric (B):** for dinosaur skin shadows

- **Blue fabric (C):** for suit

- **Dark blue fabric (D):** for lapels

- **Darkest blue fabric (E):** for shadows on suit and dinosaur claw shadows

- **Red fabric (F):** for curtain

- **Dark red fabric (G):** for curtain shadows

- **Brown background fabric (H):** 24″ × 28″

  Fabric details will be fused to this base "canvas." The 24″ × 28″ rectangle provides 2″ all around for stapling your portrait to a canvas stretcher. The fabric piece may need to be larger depending on your canvas stretcher instructions. Note that the portrait itself is 20″ × 24″.

- **Dark brown fabric (I):** for shadows and space in lower left beneath table

- **Gold fabric (J):** for dinosaur eye, armillary sphere, suit buttons, and cufflinks

- **Orange fabric (K):** for armillary sphere

- **Lilac fabric (L):** for dress shirt

- **Medium purple fabric (M):** for tie

- **Dark lilac fabric (N):** for dress shirt shadows

- **Gray fabric (O):** for tabletop

- **Tan fabric (P):** for table legs

- **White fabric (Q):** for dinosaur teeth and reflective highlights

- **Caramel brown fabric (R):** for table engravings

- **Dark plum fabric (S):** for tie shadows

- **Paper-backed fusible webbing:** approximately 1½ yards of 17″-wide webbing

- **Vintage picture frame:** 20″ × 24″

- **Canvas stretcher:** for 20″ × 24″ frame

Tip Here's a great opportunity to go wild and crazy with your fabric selections. Think about using mottled, swirly, marbleized or texture-patterned fabrics to make your portrait look that much more "painterly"! And don't stop there, because this is the perfect time to raid your stash for dashing ensemble combinations. Floral tie? Gingham dress shirt? Pinstriped suit? Why yes, don't mind if we do!

It's Go Time!

1. Using the color key (at right) as a guide, trace all patterns for a single color fabric onto a piece of paper-backed fusible webbing. You can trace the patterns close together; just leave enough room for easy cutting. Note that the patterns are in reverse, so when the fusible-backed pieces are traced and added to the background fabric, they'll appear correctly in the finished portrait.

2. Fuse webbing to the selected fabric.

3. Cut out each piece along the pencil lines. Peel away and remove the backing. Set the pieces aside.

Color key

4. Repeat Steps 1–3 for each fabric.

5. Place the background fabric on your ironing board. Using the color key as a guide, begin placing and layering all portrait pieces. You may want to lightly tack pieces in place as you layer.

All Together Now

When everything is where you'd like it, iron to fuse all the pieces together. Take extra care in heavily layered areas; make sure that everything gets well fused.

> **Tip** I chose not to finish any of my appliqué edges, as this will be a decorative wallhanging. But if you want that added treatment, feel free to topstitch around all the edges.

Almost Done!

1. Use a staple gun to mount the finished dinosaur portrait to the canvas stretcher, following the manufacturer's instructions.

> **Tip** If you feel your ode to dinosaurs is better suited for a quilt top, by all means, make it so! Make sure to topstitch around every edge, for washing durability, and then simply panel this bad boy into the center of any pieced quilt. Or make multiple dinosaur panels in different shirts and ties for one giant quilting masterpiece. The options are endless!

2. The stretched portrait is now ready to put into the vintage frame. Depending on the frame, there are different styles of framing

hardware available at framing shops. Decide which works best for the type of frame you have and consult your local shop for additional help.

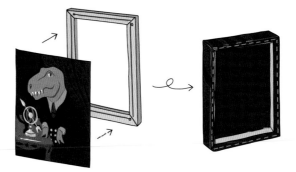

Ta-Dah!

Congratulations! You have just appliquéd your way into the hearts of art historians and paleontologists worldwide. Surely even Rembrandt would approve. With this T-Rex-cellent creation worthy of prime mantle positioning, you've done dinosaur-loving people across the land proud with this perfect prehistoric portrait.

Quilts

Fabrics

Candy Dots

Finished quilt: 56½″ × 84½″ • Finished block: 14″ × 14″

Hold onto your hats, good people. (You *do* wear a jaunty chapeau while quilting, don't you?) Do you like candy? Puh-leeze, like I even need you to answer that. I can see it in your eyes. Well, get ready to drop your surely cavity-free jaw, because this project is a retro candy classic pumped full of Claes Oldenburg and Coosje van Bruggen (I'll wait while you Google them) levels of oversized goodness. In quilt form, of course. Not only is this a madly gigantic strip of candy dots (dots, buttons; buttons, dots—call them what you want), but it's also big enough to candy-coat yourself in for bedtime. Did someone say, "Sweet dreams"?

fun facts

Many dentists say if you're gonna do it, it's better to eat a giant wad of candy in one sitting than to eat smaller portions over a longer period. Why? Eating a greater quantity at one time gives saliva more concentrated time to wash away the enamel-eroding acids that candy brings. Plus, gobs of sticky leftover candy bits clinging to teeth tend to spur more people to brushing immediately, versus smaller stints of snacking, which add up but don't compel us to good oral hygiene. How's that for being fully brushed up on your saliva-related dental knowledge?

What You'll Need

Yardage is based on fabric with 42" usable width.

- **Turquoise fabric:**
  1⅝ yards

  Cut 12 circles 10½"
  in diameter.

- **Yellow fabric:** ⅝ yard

  Cut 4 circles 10½"
  in diameter.

- **Pink fabric:** 1¼ yards

  Cut 8 circles 10½"
  in diameter.

- **White fabric:** 8¼ yards for
  background, circle lining,
  and binding

  Cut 24 squares 14½" × 14½".

  Cut 24 circles 10½"
  in diameter.

  Cut 8 strips 2" × width
  of fabric.

- **Samarra's Lunchboxes
  fabric:** 5¼ yards
  for backing

   Cut into 2 lengths
  2⅝ yards each.

- **Batting:** 65" × 93"

- **Stuffing or batting:**
  for dots

It's Go Time!

Seam allowances are ¼" for this project.

1. Place a colored dot circle and a white lining circle face to face and pin.

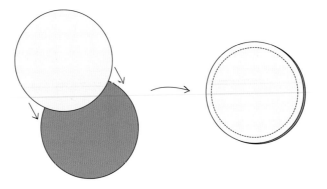

2. Sew the entire circle closed. Snip into the seam allowance all the way around to help create smooth curving.

3. Cut a 2" opening in the center of the white lining circle, making sure not to cut into the other circle side.

4. Using that opening, turn the entire circle right side out, and iron the edges flat.

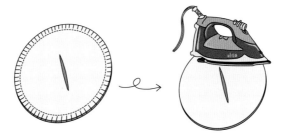

5. Fill the circle with stuffing, adding more or less based on personal preference.

Repeat Steps 1–5 to make a total of 24 colored dots.

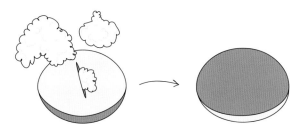

Tip

You can stuff each dot like this for added hilarity, or you might prefer to simply add a double layer of batting, which will give a little bit of a bump instead.

6. Decide whether the quilt will be finished at home or sent to a longarm quilter. If completed at home, set all stuffed circles aside. Assemble the 24 white squares to create a quilt top with 6 rows of 4 squares each. Sandwich the quilt top with the batting and backing; then quilt (see Almost Done!, page 90). Afterward, hand stitch each stuffed dot to the center of each quilted square (see All Together Now, page 90). Bind the quilt (see The Ties That Bind, page 121) to complete it.

If the quilt will be sent to a longarm quilter, as mine was, continue on with the following steps.

7. Center a stuffed circle on a white square of fabric, ensuring that the color side of the dot is facing up. Pin in place.

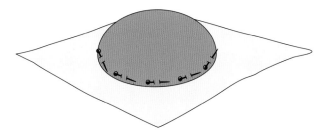

8. Topstitch all the way around the circle edge to attach it to the white square.

Repeat Steps 7 and 8 for the remaining 23 circles.

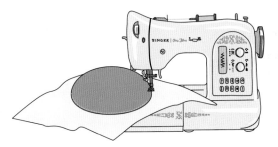

Tip

Consider using a complementary thread color for added interest. Plus, if you ever really have examined candy dots, some of them are slightly swirled and off-color because the main three colors have inadvertently mixed in production. This candy observation probably leaves you thinking I must have too much time on my hands, right? Probably, but this is why I'm an asset to any trivia party.

All Together Now

Working from the top to bottom of the quilt, sew the finished squares together, using this finished quilt diagram as a guide.

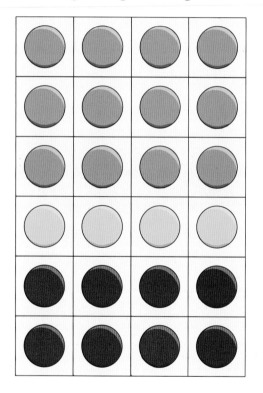

Almost Done!

1. Join the 2 pieces of backing fabric and trim to 65″ × 93″ (see Back It Up!, page 120).

2. Sandwich the assembled quilt top, batting, and backing fabric, and pin baste all layers securely in place (see Who Wants a Sandwich?, page 120).

3. Quilt and bind (see The Ties That Bind, page 121).

Ta-Dah!

Guess what? You're done! Get your jammies on, brush your pegs (that's Australian for "brush your teeth"), and get into your sweet, sweet candy dot bed. Lights out, Sugar!

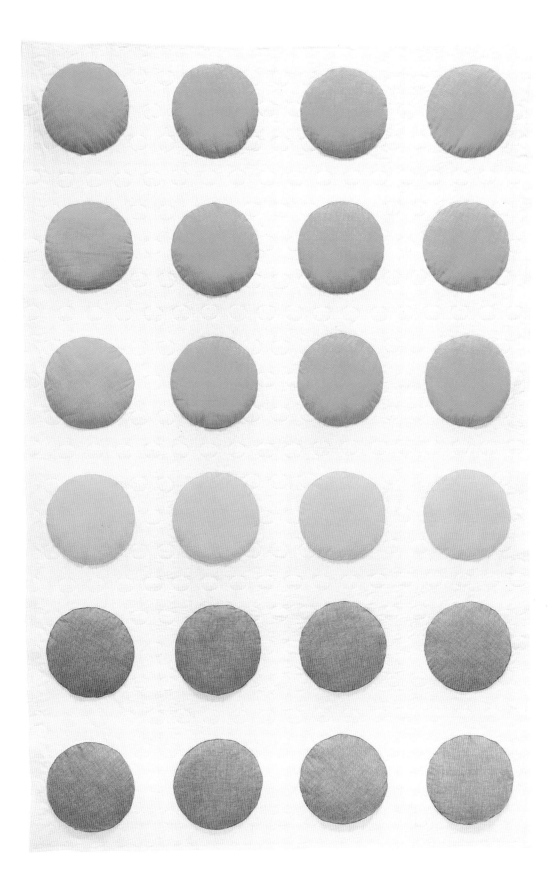

Odd Socks

Finished quilt: 38″ × 38″

Some mysteries will forever haunt time. What happened to Amelia Earhart? Who killed JFK? Why are Einstein's eyeballs being kept in an undisclosed safety deposit box long after his death? But more importantly, who ate my chocolate? Where's the other sock in this pair? … I said, Where. Is. The. Other. Sock?!?!?! Now *that's* a question for the ages. Do they gather under cover of darkness in empty parks to laugh boisterously about their newfound freedom from twindependence? Do they tell harrowing tales of long-plotted laundry room escapes while intermittently ribbing each other about their well-worn soles and frayed holes? Darn them. Darn them all. Let's not dwell on the unanswerable and instead quilt our troubles away with the *Odd Socks* throw.

 fun facts

Feet are one of the highest producers of sweat (oh, those crazy overachievers), and socks not only absorb that sweat, but also keep tootsies from getting frostbitten in winter. The word sock comes from the Latin soccus, a loose-fitting slipper once worn by Roman comic actors for added hilarity. Really. I promise I'm not making that up. Anyway, I can only guess that they helped absorb stage-fright-induced sweat as well.

The oldest pair of socks still in existence date back to 300–500 AD Egypt. And guess what, they're still a pair. Now would you look at that—right when we had almost lost all hope for sock monogamy.

What You'll Need

Yardage is based on fabric with 42″ of usable width, unless otherwise noted.

- **Blue fabric:** 1¼ yards for background

    Cut 1 square approximately 38″ × 38″.

- **White-on-cream striped fabric:** about 1 yard for socks

- **Multicolor fabrics:** for sock stripes

- **Samarra's Hidden Ladybugs fabric:** 1¼ yards of 44″–45″-wide fabric for backing

     Cut 1 square 45″ × 45″.

- **Black-and-white striped fabric:** ⅜ yard for binding

    Cut 4 strips 2″ × width of fabric.

- **Batting:** 45″ × 45″

- **Paper-backed fusible webbing**

- **Embellishments (optional):** such as beads, buttons, ribbon, and trim

It's Go Time!

All seam allowances are ¼″ for this project.

1. Go to your sock drawer and find a variety of socks of different shapes—as well as shapes and sizes from every member of the family. This is a good time to show some love to any solo socks wistfully hanging around.

Note: You will make templates from the socks, not sew them into your quilt. So socks still in pairs can return to their waiting mate.

2. Using the blue fabric square as the background, lay out all the socks, arranging them evenly on the square. To allow adequate space around the outside edges, consider your working space about 36″ × 36″ square.

Also note: Your finished quilt will not look like mine. So take this opportunity to have fun placing and spacing all the socks to your liking. You may use more or fewer socks or different types of socks.

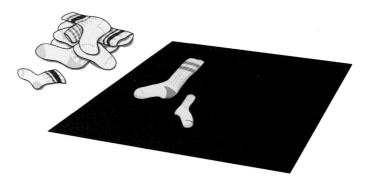

3. Trace each sock *in reverse* onto paper-backed fusible webbing. Trace stripes for each fabric onto webbing.

4. Iron webbing templates for socks to the wrong side of the white-on-cream striped fabric. Iron webbing templates for stripes to the wrong side of the various accent fabrics.

Note: This is a good time to invade your fabric stash for accents and embellishments.

5. Cut out the sock shapes and stripes.

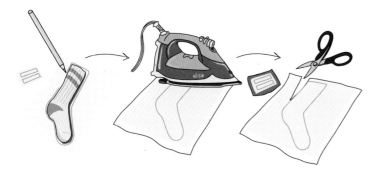

6. Position all the fabric-cut socks onto the blue background; pin in place.

7. Fuse socks to the blue background, removing pins as you iron before applying heat (unless they are heat-safe pins).

All Together Now

1. Position and iron all stripes, accents, and embellishments into place on each sock. I used a free-form approach to this, intentionally misaligning stripes to enhance the overall wonky feel.

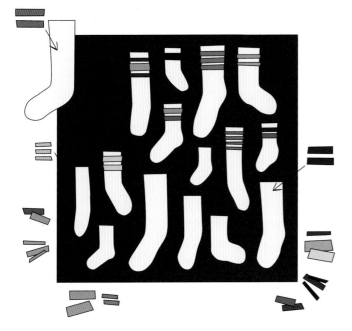

2. Use a thicker-gauge sewing thread to sew a wide satin-stitched line at the toe of each sock for added fun. Curve this line to contour to each sock's toe shape. Trim and tie off any loose threads.

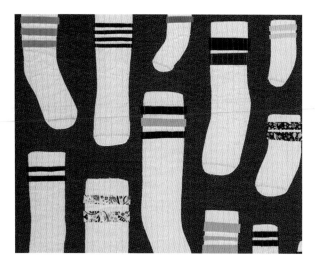

Tip Use accent fabrics for all the sock details and embellishments. Consider adding more texture and interest with ribbons, trim, or decorative machine stitches. Beads and buttons can even be used, but add those after you've completed the final quilting, as they could damage your sewing machine.

Almost Done!

1. Sandwich the assembled quilt top, batting, and backing fabric. Pin baste all layers securely in place (see Who Wants a Sandwich?, page 120).

2. Use white thread to topstitch a straight stitch all the way around each sock. Consider topstitching around all stripes—and embellishments too—to prevent future detaching.

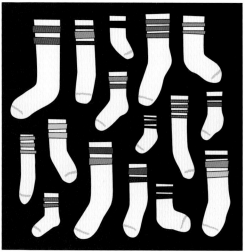

Tip For the topstitching, I chose a straight stitch because I want the raw edges to eventually fray and have a worn feel to them. If you prefer otherwise, use a narrow, compact zigzag stitch to further reinforce all the edges.

To add a fun ribbed-sock illusion to each sock, use a vertical, edge-to-edge straight stitch for your quilting, spaced anywhere from ¼˝ to ½˝ apart, depending on your sock size and overall layout.

3. Quilt and bind (see The Ties that Bind, page 121).

Ta-Dah!

And there we have it. Perhaps this will reduce the urges to rearrange
your sock drawer and lessen the chronic pain of odd sock loss. This
heirloom quilt will comfort generations to come, even as we hold out
hope that those lost "soles" will surefootedly find their way home.
But you know, don't hold your breath for that.

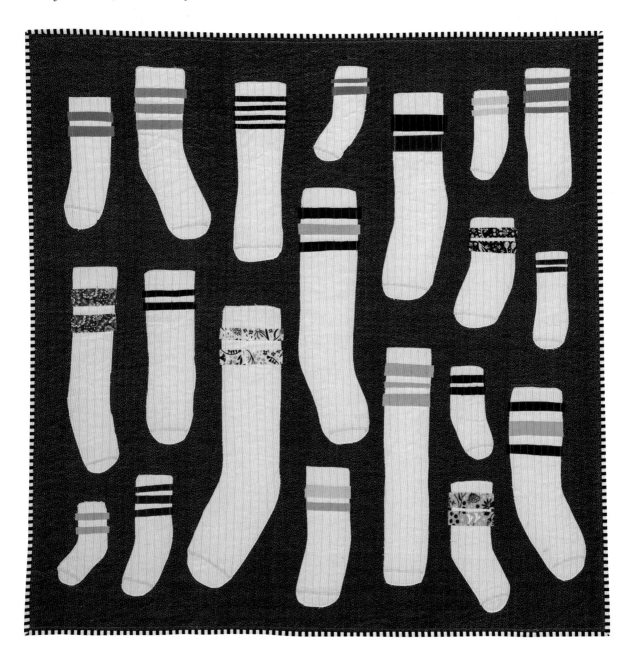

Calculator

Finished quilt: 71″ × 94½″

Here's another perfect opportunity to add an unexpected twist to a modern quilt design. Sure, up close it's a nice set of bold, graphic blocks that sew up easily, but H-E-L-L-O, it's also a comically oversized calculator! Place it on a bed to give the soon-to-be-snoozer an added surprise with a right-side-up-to-them bedtime greeting, delivered in classic school numeric calculator form.

fun facts

Because I know you're the discerning type, I'm sure we've pondered this exact same thing: Why are calculator and telephone keypads ordered in reverse to one another? Nobody knows for sure, but there are a few theories out there. Some pinpoint the need to slow user's dialing ability to align with telephone tone-recognition technology. Sounds good, but that's assuming a lot of quick calculating folks are out there. Some think the telephone keypad was adapted to transition more easily from its rotary predecessor. Others think that the specific ordering of the phone keypad helped eliminate quick finger dialing errors and that the designers purposely ignored the already-established keypad of its calculator cousin completely. That's okay, calculator. We won't ignore you like that, not to worry.

What You'll Need

Yardages are based on fabric with usable width of 42".

- **Calculator lettering patterns** (pages 104 and 105)

- **Gray fabric:** 4 yards for background

  Cut 19 rectangles 4½" × 10½" for horizontal sashing (A).

  Cut 4 rectangles 6¼" × 10½" for bottom sashing (A1).

  Cut 3 strips 5½" × 76¼" for vertical sashing (A2).

  Cut 1 strip 6¼" × 55½" for top border (A3).

  Cut 2 strips 8¼" × 94½" for side borders (A4).

- **Light gray fabric:** 1½ yards for keys

  Cut 14 squares 10½" × 10½" (B).

- **Dark gray or black fabric:** 1 fat quarter or scrap piece for key

  Cut 1 square 10½" × 10½" (C).

- **Orange fabric:** ½ yard for keys

  Cut 3 squares 10½" × 10½" (D).

- **Red fabric:** ½ yard for key

  Cut 1 rectangle 10½" × 24½" (E).

- **Turquoise fabric:** ⅞ yard for screen

  Cut 2 rectangles 13" × 29" (F).

- **Black fabric:** ⅝ yard for numbers and binding

  Reserve ⅞ yard for numbers.

  Cut 9 strips 2" × width of fabric.

- **Samarra's Mathematics fabric:** 5¾ yards for backing

  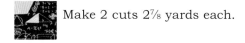 Make 2 cuts 2⅞ yards each.

- **Batting:** 79" × 103"

- **Paper-backed fusible webbing**

It's Go Time

All seam allowances are ¼" for this project.

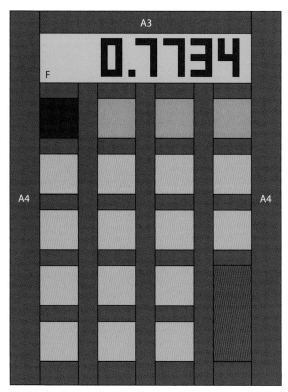

Finished calculator

1. Setting aside border pieces A3 and A4 and turquoise piece F, use the keypad layout diagrams below as your guide as you stitch together all columns of the calculator keypad.

2. Take all assembled columns and stitch them into a single unit, incorporating the vertical sashing pieces (A2) in between. Set aside.

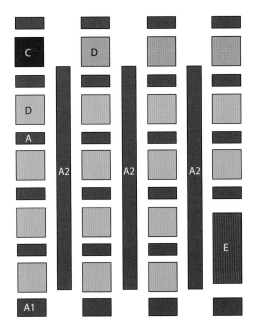

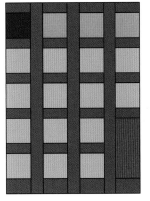

Keypad layout

3. Trace patterns for lettering onto paper-backed fusible webbing.

Note: The patterns are in reverse so that the pieces will be correctly oriented for fusing to the background (Step 6).

4. Adhere fusible webbing to the back of the black fabric. Carefully cut out each digit, using a rotary cutter where possible. Use scissors for precise cutting of inside corners.

5. Join 2 turquoise rectangles at a short end to make a strip about 13″ × 57½″. With the seam in the center, trim the piece to 13″ × 55½″ (rectangle F).

6. Remove the paper backing from the letters. Using the screen layout diagram below as your guide, place the digits face up on the turquoise rectangle F. Iron to securely fuse them in place.

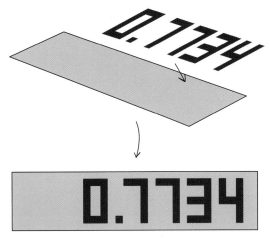

Screen layout

7. For a finished look, use black thread to topstitch around the edges of each digit. I used a satin stitch.

Tip

In my 1980s world growing up, it was a classic move to type out H-E-L-L-O on one's calculator. I was too much of a Goody Two-shoes to even realize there were more racy things one could spell. So if you want to mix things up and go for something more bawdy, feel free!

All Together Now

1. Attach turquoise rectangle F (the screen) to the top of the assembled keypad.

2. Add top border A3 to the top of rectangle F. This completes the center section of your calculator.

3. Add side borders A4 to each side of the keypad screen piece. Iron all seams open.

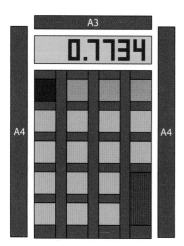

Almost Done!

1. Join cut lengths of backing fabric and trim to make a 79″ × 103″ piece (see Back It Up!, page 120).

2. Sandwich the assembled quilt top, batting, and backing fabric. Then pin baste all layers securely in place (see Who Wants a Sandwich?, page 120).

3. Quilt and bind (see The Ties That Bind, page 121).

Ta-Dah!

According to my calculations, we can now call this number complete! Adding a large, unabashed, comedic layer of dorky fun to a modern quilt approach totals mathematical genius—if we do say so ourselves. And H-E-L-L-O! That so totally *does* compute!

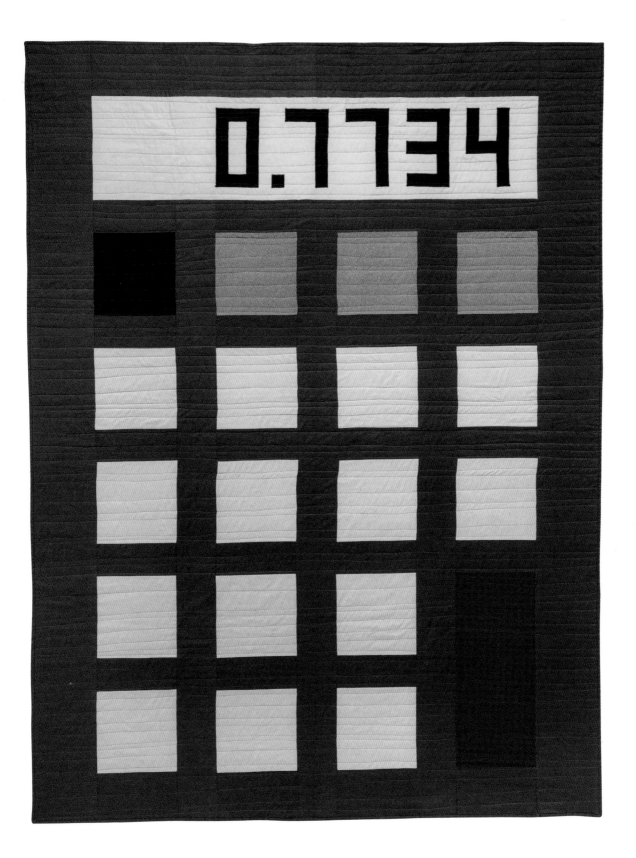

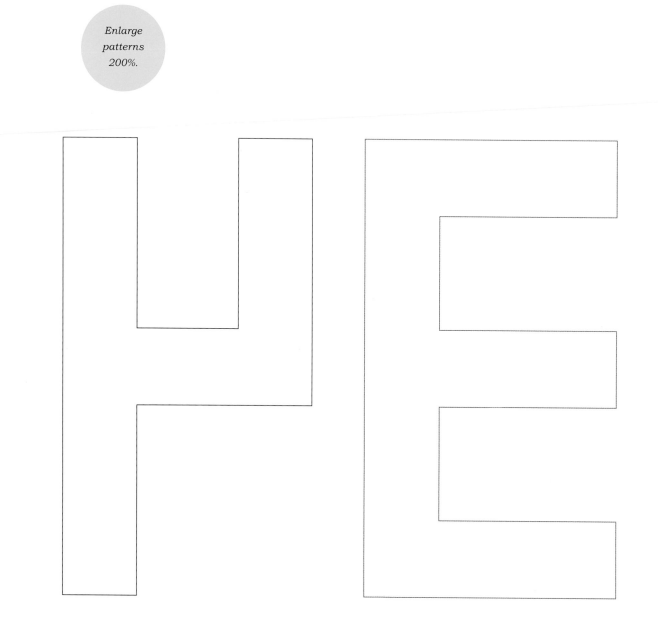

Enlarge patterns 200%.

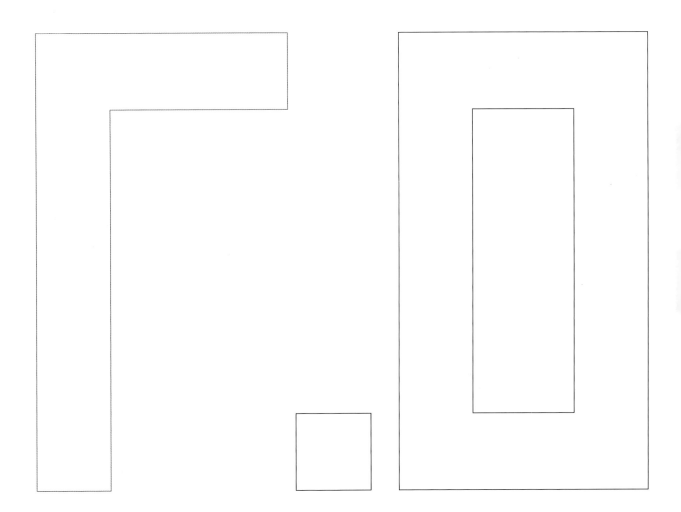

8-Bit Birds

Finished quilt: 60½″ × 60½″

It's time to get old school, ladies and gents. Not only are we going to hop into a time capsule and get all early 1980s on this place, but we're also going to slow down the pace and call for a gazillion squares to be cut, in keeping with this binary, block-based graphics theme. You may choose to short-cut things and introduce larger background squares of fabric, but this is the perfect time to take the slow road and embrace going the long way around. Like we did in the '80s when we had to walk twenty miles barefoot in the snow to get to the nearest video game arcade. Okay, fine, not really. We carpooled in a wood-paneled station wagon. But you get my point.

fun facts

Mallards are called "dabbling" ducks because they tip their entire bodies forward into the water to reach food. I highly suggest everyone try this at the dinner table sometime.

Blue jays are not only aggressive and intelligent birds (lethal combo), but they also like to go "anting." You know, picking up ants and rubbing them all over their birdie bodies, ostensibly to handle feather molting and parasites or to make the ant more edible after rubbing its harmful acids away. This, good people, I do not suggest trying at the dinner table, unless you plan on never seeing your fellow diners again. In that case, go for the gold.

The Northern Cardinal has the greedy distinction of being the most chosen state bird, representing seven—count 'em, seven—states: Illinois, Indiana, Kentucky, North Carolina, Ohio, Virginia, and West Virginia. No wonder blue jays are grumpy hotheads.

What You'll Need

Yardages are based on fabric with usable width of 42".

- **Off-white fabric (A):**
3⅞ yards for background and binding

  Cut 732 squares 2½" × 2½".

  Cut 7 strips 2" × width of fabric.

  (*Note:* This fabric should be dense or heavy enough that dark seam allowances won't show through it.)

For mallard:

- **Orange fabric (B):**
⅛ yard or scrap pieces

  Cut 5 squares 2½" × 2½".

- **Medium green fabric (C):**
⅛ yard or scrap pieces

  Cut 5 squares 2½" × 2½".

- **Dark green fabric (D):**
⅛ yard or scrap pieces

  Cut 3 squares 2½" × 2½".

- **Pale gray fabric (E):**
scrap pieces

  Cut 2 squares 2½" × 2½".

- **Dark brown fabric (F):**
¼ yard

  Cut 17 squares 2½" × 2½".

- **Medium brown fabric (G):**
⅛ yard

  Cut 11 squares 2½" × 2½".

- **Tan fabric (H):** ⅛ yard

  Cut 8 squares 2½" × 2½".

- **Medium gray fabric (I):**
⅛ yard or scrap pieces

  Cut 4 squares 2½" × 2½".

- **Light brown fabric (J):**
⅛ yard

  Cut 7 squares 2½" × 2½".

For cardinal:

- **Bright yellow fabric (K):**
⅛ yard

  Cut 5 squares 2½" × 2½"

- **Black fabric (L):**
scrap pieces

  Cut 3 squares 2½" × 2½"

- **Bright red fabric (M):**
¼ yard

  Cut 27 squares 2½" × 2½"

- **Medium red fabric (N):**
scrap pieces

  Cut 2 squares 2½" × 2½".

- **Dark red fabric (O):**
⅛ yard

  Cut 15 squares 2½" × 2½".

For blue jay:

- **Medium gray fabric (P):**
⅛ yard

  Cut 5 squares 2½" × 2½".

- **Black fabric (Q):** ⅛ yard

  Cut 10 squares 2½" × 2½".

- **Navy blue fabric (R):**
scrap pieces

  Cut 2 squares 2½" × 2½".

- **Bright blue fabric (S):**
⅛ yard or scrap pieces

  Cut 4 squares 2½" × 2½".

- **Medium blue fabric (T):**
⅛ yard

  Cut 13 squares 2½" × 2½".

- **Turquoise fabric (U):**
⅛ yard

  Cut 8 squares 2½" × 2½".

- **Light blue fabric (V):**
⅛ yard

  Cut 12 squares 2½" × 2½".

(Whew! Almost ran out of alphabet there!)

- **Samarra's Subway Map fabric:** 4 yards for backing

  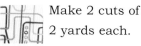 Make 2 cuts of 2 yards each.

- **Batting:** 69" × 69"

Tip

Feel free to let your creative urges run free! Raid your fabric stash for the birds, especially where small quantities of fabric are needed. The colors don't have to be exact, though the tonal differences are important for delineating the details of specific birds. If you're so inclined, you can even make up your own birds, real or imagined! Show off that rare Northeastern Plum-Billed Goosefinch you just discovered in your dreams!

It's Go Time!

All seam allowances are ¼" for this project.

1. Cut out all squares.

2. Using the quilt piecing diagram as your guide, assemble squares into 30 rows.

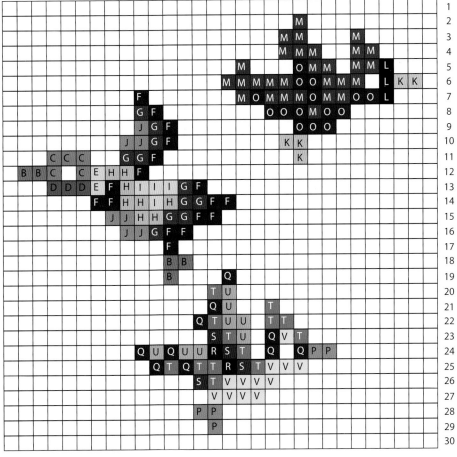

Quilt piecing

3. After completing a row, iron each square's allowance in that row in an alternating direction from its neighboring square. When the second row is complete, iron those alternating allowances in the reverse direction to the row above. Doing this creates a locking system within pieced rows, so that they are much easier to align and sew together, ensuring that all corners match up on point.

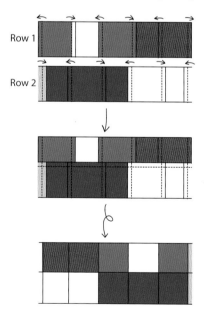

All Together Now

After the rows are pieced, assemble them using the quilt piecing diagram (page 109) as your guide.

Almost Done!

1. Iron the fully assembled quilt top so that all seams lie flat.

2. Join cut lengths of backing fabric and trim to make a 69″ × 69″ piece (see Back It Up!, page 120).

3. Sandwich the assembled quilt top, batting, and backing fabric; then pin baste all layers securely in place (see Who Wants a Sandwich?, page 120).

4. Starting in the middle of one side of your quilt, begin stitching in-the-ditch from one side to the other along each row of your quilt. Work out from the center, and start the edge-to-edge sewing from the same edge.

5. Once rows are stitched, repeat Step 4 for each column. Starting in the middle of a top or bottom quilt edge, stitch in-the-ditch along each column. Work outward to create an overall grid pattern that accentuates each bird pixel square.

6. Bind and finish (see The Ties That Bind, page 121).

Ta-Dah!

No need to migrate in the winter now. Your *8-Bit Birds* throw is complete and ready to nest in all season long! Now that's something to crow about, my fine feathered friends.

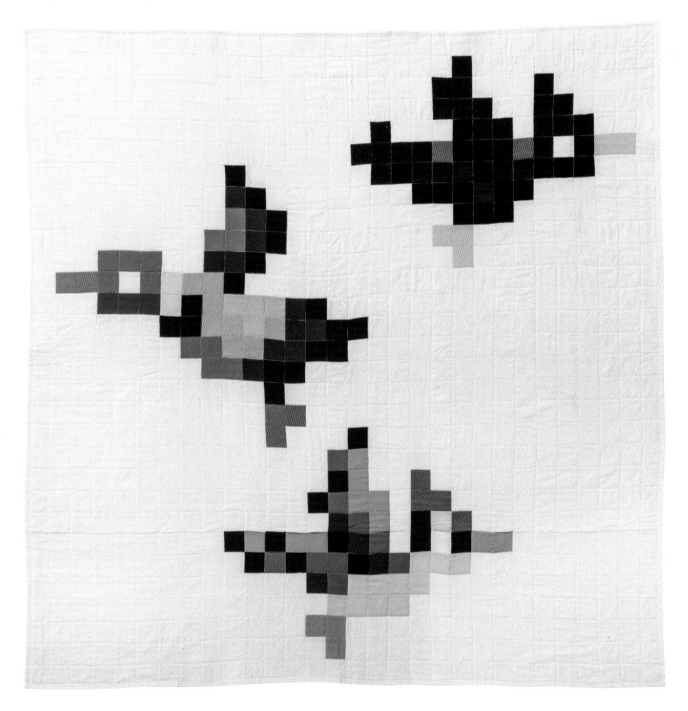

Braille Alphabet

Finished quilt: 84½″ × 105½″ • Finished block: 14″ × 21″

In elementary school, I ordered *Louis Braille: The Boy Who Invented Books for the Blind* from one of the Scholastic book flyers. When it arrived, I was completely enraptured, my child brain racing with thoughts of what it must have been like for a kid like me to once have sight and then lose it. I had no idea at the time what an *awl* was, but I swore to myself that I'd never go near one. Still, fascinated, I'd spend hours running my fingers over the alphabet that was embossed into the back cover of my paperback copy. All these years later, it's still one of my favorite examples of typography, seamlessly combining form and function into straightforward clean design. What better way to admire its inherent beauty than to showcase it in a bold, modern quilt? … I knew you'd agree.

fun facts

Braille becomes even more beautiful when you can decode its pattern. Look closely and you'll see that the entire alphabet is based on a basic set of ten dot configurations. Those are seen in A through J. K through T repeats that set of ten dot configurations and adds one additional dot to the lower left corner of each cell. U through Z repeats the K through T sequencing and adds one additional dot to the lower right of each cell. Pretty neat stuff! But hang on a second, why does W not follow that pattern? I thought you'd never ask. The letter W does not exist in French—Braille's original language—so it was never included. It was later added to fulfill the English need for the letter. Overall, it's a perfect example of my favorite type of pure-practical, no-frills, ingeniously simple-seeming and yet completely world-expanding design.… Can you tell I love Braille?

What You'll Need

Yardages are based on fabric with usable width of 42", unless otherwise noted.

- **Off-white fabric:** 6½ yards 44"–45"-wide fabric for background

  Cut 30 rectangles 14½" × 21½".

- **Samarra's Stained Glass Rose Windows fabric:**
  9⅔ yards 44"–45" fabric for backing

   Divide into 3 equal cuts
  (about 116" × width of fabric each).

- **Batting:** 93" × 114"

- **Tear-away fusible stabilizer:** 14 yards (from 15"-wide roll)

  Cut 180 squares 5½" × 5½".

For Braille dot letters, gather enough fabric pieces to cut out the required number of 5"-diameter circles (see It's Go Time!, Step 1, next page).

- **A—Light blue:** 1 circle
- **B—Light purple:** 2 circles
- **C—Pink:** 2 circles
- **D—Bright pink:** 3 circles
- **E—Orange:** 2 circles
- **F—Red:** 3 circles
- **G—Dark purple:** 4 circles
- **H—Navy blue:** 3 circles
- **I—Royal blue:** 2 circles
- **J—Aqua blue:** 3 circles
- **K—Dark green:** 2 circles
- **L—Lime green:** 3 circles

- **M—Bright yellow:** 3 circles
- **N—Yellow-orange:** 4 circles
- **O—Curry:** 3 circles
- **P—Chocolate brown:** 4 circles
- **Q—Dark gray:** 5 circles
- **R—Medium gray:** 4 circles
- **S—Blue-gray:** 3 circles
- **T—Lilac:** 4 circles
- **U—Deep pink:** 3 circles
- **V—Ruby red:** 4 circles

- **W—Coral red:** 4 circles
- **X—Peach:** 4 circles
- **Y—Turquoise:** 5 circles
- **Z—Sage green:** 4 circles
- **Paper-backed fusible webbing:** about 4½ yards (17" wide) for 84 fabric circles
- **Template paper:** Cut a 5"-diameter circle template.

It's Go Time!

All seam allowances are ¼″ for this project.

1. Iron fusible webbing to the back of all letter fabrics. Use the 5″-diameter circle template (see What You'll Need, previous page) to cut out the required circles. Set aside.

2. Fold a 14½″ × 21½″ off-white rectangle in half lengthwise. Iron the fold flat.

3. Open the rectangle again and fold it in thirds widthwise, with the first fold 7¼″ from the top and the second fold 7¼″ from the bottom (see folding diagram). Iron all folds flat.

4. Open the rectangle again. It will now have a 6-box grid. This is the letter "cell" upon which each alphabet letter will be created.

5. Repeat Steps 2–4 to create a total of 30 creased rectangle cells.

6. Refer to the finished quilt diagram (at right). Starting with the letter A, peel the fusible backing from a pale blue circle. Visually center the circle in the top left box, keeping in mind that this box has a ¼″ seam allowance on the top and left side. Iron the circle in place.

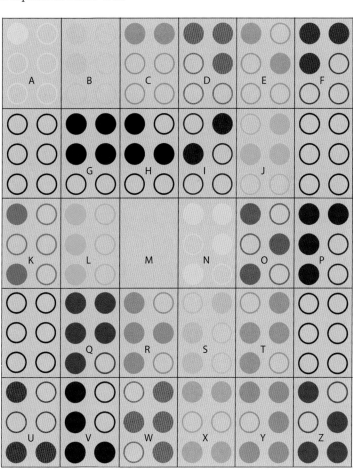

Finished quilt

7. Use the circle template to draw a 5″-diameter circle on the right side of the fabric in the center of each remaining box, also taking into account the ¼″ seam allowance around the rectangle cell's outer edges. **A**

8. Flip over the rectangle cell and apply a 5½″ × 5½″ square of tear-away fusible stabilizer to the back of each box, centering the stabilizer on each 5″ circle. **B**

9. Turn the rectangle cell right side up. Use matching pale blue thread to satin stitch completely around the pale blue fabric circle.

10. Satin stitch over each of the remaining drawn circles. **C**

11. Tear away all the fusible stabilizer from the back of the rectangle cell. Iron the rectangle cell flat.

12. Repeat Steps 6–11 with alphabet letters B–Z, using the finished quilt diagram (page 115) for specific circle placement. Remember to take the seam allowances into account when you place the circles! Be sure to use 26 unique thread colors that coordinate with each fabric used for the 26 letter circles.

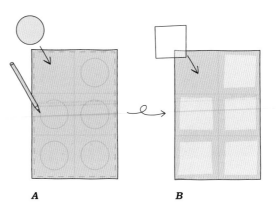

A   *B*

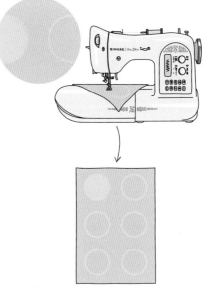

C

All Together Now

Repeat It's Go Time, Steps 7, 8, 10, and 11 (previous page), to create 4 blank cells, each with 6 circles, 5″ in diameter. Use black thread to satin stitch on the circle outlines. These cells will be placed at the beginning and end of the second and fourth rows of the quilt.

Almost Done!

1. Assemble the finished rectangles together in rows, from left to right, as follows:

Row 1: A, B, C, D, E, F

Row 2: Blank cell, G, H, I, J, blank cell

Row 3: K, L, M, N, O, P

Row 4: Blank cell, Q, R, S, T, blank cell

Row 5: U, V, W, X, Y, Z

2. Sew all rows together, using the finished quilt diagram (page 115) as a guide.

3. Sew together the 3 cuts of backing and cut to make a 93″ × 114″ piece (see Back It Up!, page 120).

4. Sandwich the assembled quilt top, batting, and pieced backing; pin baste all layers securely in place (see Who Wants a Sandwich?, page 120).

5. Quilt your sandwich! For mine, I chose to accentuate each letter cell a little further by quilting a circle around each colored Braille dot to give them an embossed feel, while making the remaining empty dots recede into the cell background more by incorporating them into the background quilting.

6. Bind the quilt (see The Ties That Bind, page 121).

Ta-Dah!

Braille may have been invented more than 200 years ago, but it sure does make for a perfectly modern, graphic, and bold quilt today. Not only is it pretty to look at, but it's also full of meaning, making it a perfect educational tool. So make many and spread the word, letter by letter!

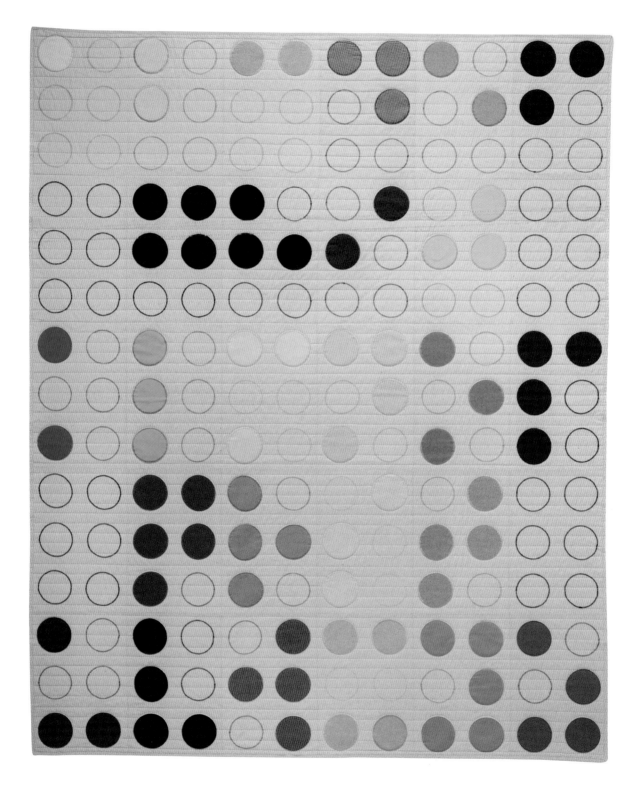

Hey, How'd Ya Do That?

Devil in the Details

Prewashing

I prewash all fabrics for my clothing projects. Where shrinking is a crucial factor, I want to nip it in the bud before doing any measuring or cutting. I do not, however, like to prewash anything for decorative projects or quilts. There. I said it. Maybe I'm a freak for how fabric handles and feels right off the bolt; it's just much more manageable to me. I also loathe ironing giant swaths of fabric. Little bits and pieces, okay. Waves and waves of yardage, no. Not unless I want to bring myself to tears and feel an inappropriate knee-jerk reaction to set all of it on fire in the backyard. Don't do that. Never do that. Rather, decide how you like to work best, and pick the method that suits you, given all the advantages and pitfalls either route offers.

Seam Allowances

A ¼″ seam allowance is used for most quilt projects. It's a good idea to do a test seam before you begin sewing to check that your ¼″ is accurate. Accuracy is the key to successful piecing.

Nonquilted projects generally utilize a ½″ or ⅝″ seam allowance.

There is generally no need to backstitch. Seamlines will be crossed by another seam, which will anchor them.

Pressing

In general, it's best to press seams toward the darker fabric. However, when assembling many same-size pieces, it can be very helpful to alternate the direction of your seams. Alternating directions helps each section interlock with the next. Always be sure to bring your iron straight down on your fabric, pressing and lifting lightly in an up-and-down motion. Don't "scrub" your iron to and fro (just press!), because that will warp and distort your fabric. Save your comically over-the-top ironing for a round of charades. Avoid using a very hot iron and avoid over-ironing, which can distort shapes and blocks. Be especially careful when pressing bias edges, as they stretch easily.

Who Wants a Sandwich?

Back It Up!

Backing is generally specified at 4″ larger than the quilt on each side, or 8″ longer and wider than the quilt top. To make the backing large enough for the quilt, you'll often have to join two or more pieces of yardage. First, determine the edges to be joined—most likely it will be the long sides or selvage edges. Then trim off the selvages on the edges to be joined. Stitch together with a ½″ seam allowance and press the seam open. Lay the pieced lining out flat. Trim to the dimensions specified in the quilt instructions, keeping the vertical or horizontal seam(s) as close as possible to the center of the piece.

Batting

The type of batting you choose is a personal decision; consult your local quilt shop. Cut batting approximately 8″ longer and wider than your quilt top. Note that your batting choice will affect how much quilting the quilt will need. Check the manufacturer's instructions to see how far apart the quilting lines can be.

Layering

Spread the backing wrong side up and tape down the edges with masking tape. (If you are working on carpet, you can use T-pins to secure the backing to the carpet.) Center the batting on top, smoothing out any folds. Place the quilt top right side up on top of the batting and backing, making sure it is centered.

Basting

Basting keeps the quilt "sandwich" layers from shifting while you quilt.

If you plan to machine quilt, pin baste the quilt layers together with safety pins placed about 3″–4″ apart. Begin basting in the center and move toward the edges first in vertical and then horizontal rows. Try not to pin directly on the intended quilting lines.

If you plan to hand quilt, baste the layers together with thread using a long needle and light-colored thread. Knot one end of the thread. Using stitches approximately the length of the needle, begin in the center and move out toward the edges in vertical and horizontal rows, approximately 4″ apart. Add two diagonal rows of basting.

The Ties That Bind

Quilting

Quilting, whether by hand or machine, enhances the quilt's pieced or appliquéd design. You may choose to quilt in-the-ditch, echo the pieced or appliqué motifs, use patterns from quilting design books and stencils, or do your own free-motion quilting. Remember to check your batting manufacturer's recommendations for how close the quilting lines must be.

Binding

Trim excess batting and backing from the quilt even with the edges of the quilt top.

DOUBLE-FOLD STRAIGHT-GRAIN BINDING

If you want a ¼" finished binding, cut the binding strips 2" wide and piece them together with diagonal seams to make a continuous binding strip. Trim the seam allowance to ¼". Press the seams open. **A & B**

Press the entire strip in half lengthwise with wrong sides together. With raw edges even, pin the binding to the front edge of the quilt a few inches away from a corner, leaving the first few inches of the binding unattached. Start sewing, using a ¼" seam allowance.

Stop ¼" away from the first corner (**C**) and backstitch one stitch. Lift the presser foot and needle. Rotate the quilt one-quarter turn. Fold the binding at a right angle so it extends straight above the quilt and the fold forms a 45° angle in the corner (**D**). Then bring the binding strip down even with the quilt's edge (**E**). Begin sewing at the folded edge. Repeat in the same manner at all corners.

Continue stitching until you are back near the beginning of the binding strip. See Finishing the Binding Ends for tips on finishing and hiding the raw edges of the binding ends.

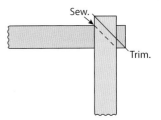

A. Sew from corner to corner.

B. Completed diagonal seam

C. Stitch to ¼" from the corner.

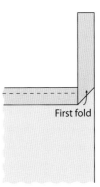

D. First fold for miter

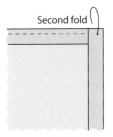

E. Second fold alignment

Finishing the Binding Ends

METHOD 1

After stitching around the quilt, fold under the beginning tail of the binding strip ¼″ so that the raw edge will be inside the binding after it is turned to the back of the quilt. Place the end tail of the binding strip over the beginning folded end. Continue to attach the binding and stitch slightly beyond the starting stitches. Trim the excess binding. Fold the binding over the raw edges to the quilt back and hand stitch, mitering the corners.

> **Tip** I used Wonder Clips (by Clover) to keep the binding in place for hand stitching. Otherwise this can easily turn into something resembling hand-to-tentacle combat with an unruly octopus. So, to cut down on your battle, little clippy friends such as these are a good ally.

METHOD 2

See the tip at ctpub.com/quilting-sewing-tips > Completing a Binding with an Invisible Seam.

Fold the ending tail of the binding back on itself where it meets the beginning binding tail. From the fold, measure and mark the cut width of your binding strip. Cut the ending binding tail to this measurement.

For example, if your binding is cut 2⅛″ wide, measure from the fold on the ending tail of the binding 2⅛″; cut the binding tail to this length. **A**

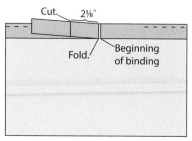

A. *Cut the binding tail.*

Open both tails. Place one tail on top of the other tail at right angles, right sides together. Mark a diagonal line from corner to corner and stitch on the line (**B**). Check that you've done it correctly and that the binding fits the quilt; then trim the seam allowance to ¼″. Press open.

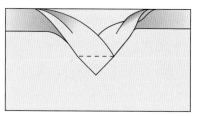

B. *Stitch the binding ends diagonally.*

Refold the binding and stitch this binding section in place on the quilt. Fold the binding over the raw edges to the quilt back and hand stitch.

Tools of the Trade*

I have used a lot of really helpful products and tools to create the projects in this book. You can certainly achieve them the sweet old-fashioned way, but if you want to increase your efficiency (Why, you're not multitasking your multitasking enough? Slow down already!), here are some of the pleasurably efficient tools I used to stop me from losing my marbles along my merry DIY way.

Aurifil   aurifil.com
Sewing and embroidery thread

AccuQuilt   accuquilt.com
Go! Fabric Cutter with square die, circle die, and 2½"-strip die

* a.k.a.
Samarra's Secret Stash of Supply Sweetness

Clover clover-usa.com
Wonder Clips, flower-head and glass-head pins, sewing needles, seam ripper, scissors

Jeannie Jenkins itchn2stitch.blogspot.com
Longarm quilting service

Dritz dritz.com
Curtain grommets, quilter's safety pins, elastic

Olfa olfa.com
Mat board, ergonomic retracting rotary cutter, square rulers

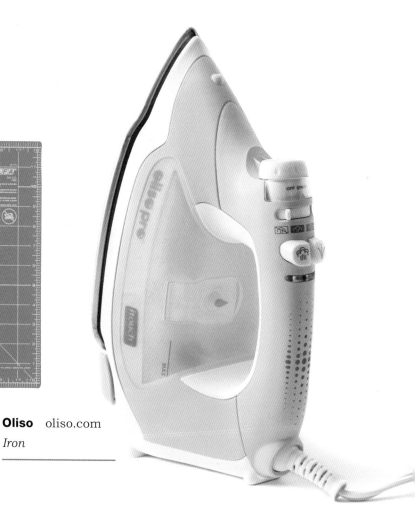

Oliso oliso.com
Iron

Pellon pellonprojects.com
*Perfect Loft stuffing, batting,
Wonder-Under fusible webbing,
Craft-Fuse, and Shape-Flex
fusible interfacings*

Timeless Treasures
ttfabrics.com
All fabrics

Wacom wacom.com
*Cintiq 13HD
interactive tablet and
stylus (I used it for
all the illustrations
in this book.)*

Singer svpworldwide.com;
singer.com
*One Plus sewing
machine and walking foot*

About the Author

Samarra Khaja:

noun—suh•MAHR•rah KAH•jah

- *First name:* Emphasis on "mar" syllable. *Last name:* The "h" is silent. Silent, but deadly. Never ignore a silent "h."

- Left handed, half-Indian, half-Australian. Has no quick answer to, "So where are you from?" Lived and traveled globally, including magical childhood stints in Australia, Dubai, and Singapore. Feels most at home in cultural melting pots like New York City.

- Schooled in fine arts, with a focus on drawing, printmaking, and photography. Also came away with a beautifully esoteric minor in medieval studies, which means she can recite the first eighteen lines of *The Canterbury Tales* in Middle English at any given moment and knows way too much about apse mosaic iconography.

- Has worked across disciplines as a designer, photographer, art director, and illustrator for the likes of *The New York Times*, The Guggenheim, Bliss (spa and skin care), *Time* magazine, Victoria's Secret, and Cirque du Soleil—all in her signature whimsical style.

- Is constantly making things or thinking about making things, because of a genetically hardwired thirst to be creative. Similar to involuntary bodily functions like heart beating and breathing.

- Aside from bolts of scrumptious fabric, other places to spot her creations in the wild include a giant 24-by-120-foot outdoor illustrated mural in Brooklyn and foolishly anthropomorphized (and oh-so-very-cheesy) food illustrations on permanent display at Kraft Foods headquarters in Chicago. And now, this book of awesomesauceness.

- Adores animals, her family, bold patterns, thrift store scores, copious amounts of chocolate, a good glass of red wine, and the color green.

- Can be followed globally at samarrakhaja.com.

Photo by Ann Pe